THE BATTLE OF
THE BULGE
1944
HITLER'S LAST HOPE

THE BATTLE OF
THE BULGE
1944
HITLER'S LAST HOPE

ROBIN CROSS

CASEMATE
HAVERTOWN, PA

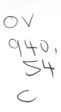

OV
940,
54
C

This edition first published in 2002 by

CASEMATE

2114 Darby Road
Havertown, PA 19083

Library of Congress Cataloging-in-Publication Data available.

ISBN: 1-932033-00-9

Editorial and design by
Amber Books Ltd
Bradley's Close
74-77 White Lion Street
London N1 9PF

Project Editor: Charles Catton
Editor: Caroline Ellerby
Design: Colin Hawes
Picture Research: Lisa Wren and Chris Bishop

Printed and bound in Italy by: Eurolitho S.p.A., Cesano Boscone (MI)

Picture credits
Ian Baxter/HITM: 36, 40 (b), 42, 59, 62, 63, 64, 68 (both), 69, 73, 78, 80, 99 (t), 106, 107, 112, 139 (b), 142, 149, 158. **POPPERFOTO**: 50, 129, 152, 154. **Suddeutscher Verlag**: 8, 13, 15, 16, 17, 18, 19, 21 (t), 24, 25, 26, 30, 33, 38, 39, 41, 44, 45, 46, 57 (both), 58, 60, 65, 70, 72, 74, 75, 77 (t), 82 (t), 83, 85, 88, 92, 105, 111, 133, 160, 167 (b). **TRH Pictures**: 6, 9, 10,11, 12, 14, 20, 21 (b), 22, 23, 28, 29, 31 (both), 32, 34, 35, 40 (t), 43, 47, 48, 51, 53, 54, 55, 56, 61, 66, 67, 76, 77 (b), 79, 81, 82 (b), 84, 86, 87, 89, 90, 95, 96, 97 (both), 98, 99 (b), 100, 101, 102, 103, 104, 108, 109, 113, 114, 116, 118, 119, 120, 121, 122, 123 (both), 124, 125 (both), 126, 127, 130, 131, 132, 134, 136, 137, 138, 139 (t), 140, 141, 143, 144 (both), 146, 147, 148, 150, 151, 155, 156, 157 (both), 159, 161, 162, 163, 164, 165, 167 (t), 168, 169, 170, 171.

Maps produced by Peter Harper

Contents

CHAPTER ONE

Lost Victories

...I believe that each of you in the hour of difficulty and danger will realize what a short second that is in the life of the earth, in the life of our Volk *[people]. And during this short second the only thing that matters is that he who lives presently there (at that time) now does his duty ...*

Heinrich Himmler, 26 July 1944

By August 1944, the Third Reich was beginning a battle for survival. Only two years before, in the spring of 1942, Nazi Germany stood at the height of its power, controlling an empire that ran from the Atlantic seaboard of France to Norway, and then south to the Russian steppe to Kharkov and the Crimea. Adolf Hitler's grand strategic plan for 1942 had envisaged a vast pincer movement driving from the Caucasus, Egypt and the Balkans that would secure the oilfields of the Middle East and in turn sustain his panzer divisions.

The Führer's dreams had turned to dust. By the summer of 1944, Hitler's horizons and ambitions had shrunk inexorably. In Western Europe the Allies had landed in Normandy on 6 June 1944, and by the end of August had surged out of their invasion bridge-head to stand on the River Seine from Troyes, 160km (100 miles) south of Paris, to the sea. Paris had been liberated on 25 August and four days later the last German troops had slipped across the Seine, leaving littered behind them in Normandy a total of 2200 destroyed or abandoned armoured vehicles, as well as a huge collection of 210,000 prisoners. The German casualties from the fighting had reached a staggering 240,000 men killed or wounded.

Left: US troops come ashore in Normandy, 6 June 1944. The success of Operation 'Overlord' in the West was matched on the Eastern Front by a renewed Red Army offensive which resulted in the destruction of German Army Group Centre in the late summer of 1944.

Three months of fighting in Normandy had cost the German Army in the West (*Westheer*) twice as many men as the battle for Stalingrad. On 20 August, 50,000 men had been trapped in the Falaise pocket, sealed off in the north by Lieutenant-General Henry Crerar's Canadian 1st Army and in the south by General George S. Patton's US 3rd Army. Two days after the Allied jaws had snapped shut, the Allied Supreme Commander, General Dwight D. Eisenhower, had toured the battlefield, encountering 'scenes that could only be described by Dante. It was literally possible to walk for hundreds of yards at a time stepping over nothing but dead and decayed flesh.' Allied aircrew flying low over these scenes wrinkled their noses in disgust at the rising stench of corpses putrefying in the late summer heat.

On the Eastern Front, Germany's strategic position in Belorussia had been reduced to ruins by the destruction of Army Group Centre in the Red Army offensive of July/August 1944. To the north, in the Baltic states of Lithuania, Latvia and Estonia, Army Group North was rolled up by three Baltic Fronts and the Leningrad Front. Tallinn fell to the Leningrad Front on 22 September and Riga was taken on 15 October. The splintering of Army Group North sent millions of refugees fleeing westwards towards the Reich or northwards to the Baltic ports. The people of the Baltic states were soon to exchange one merciless master for another. The Soviets were now within reach of the German homeland.

On 4 September, Germany's former ally, Finland, had concluded an armistice with the Soviet Union, rendering the German position in the Scandinavian theatre untenable. On the southern sector of the Eastern Front, the situation was equally grave for the German High Command. In August 1944, Romanian guerrillas had staged an armed rebellion in Bucharest, taken control of the city, arrested the puppet dictator and erstwhile German ally Marshal Ion Antonescu, and overthrown the government. King Michael had then formed a new government, negotiated an armistice with the Allies and declared war on Germany. By the end of August, most of the German occupying forces had left Romania, and on the 30th, Soviet troops entered Bucharest without meeting any armed resistance. German troops also withdrew from Bulgaria, which signed an armistice with the Soviet Union on 5 September.

Hitler's Balkan strategy was falling apart in his hands. The German occupation of Greece had been fatally undermined by the capitulation of Italy in September 1943. Just over a year later, on 12 October 1944, German Army Group E began a fighting withdrawal from Greece in order to link up with German Army Group F in Yugoslavia.

Below: Hitler and his generals on the Eastern Front in June 1942. Gazing intently at the map, and standing on the Führer's left, is General Friedrich Paulus, who several months later was to command the doomed German 6th Army at Stalingrad.

This catalogue of territorial losses dealt a severe blow to German war industry. The fruits of conquest had bestowed Romanian oil, Finnish and Norwegian nickel and copper, Swedish high-grade ore, Russian manganese, French bauxite and Spanish mercury. Now these strategic materials were either lost to the enemy or denied by cagey neutrals who could see clearly which way the war was going.

As his eyes restlessly moved over the war maps in his headquarters in Rastenburg in East Prussia, the so-called *Wolfschanze* (Wolf's Lair), Hitler could still find some crumbs of comfort. North of the Carpathians, Army Group South, which had narrowly escaped destruction in August 1944, was now holding its own in Hungary. In Italy, where Rome had fallen to the Allies on 4 June, the German 10th and 14th Armies, commanded by Field Marshal Albert Kesselring, had withdrawn behind the Gothic Line. This was a highly fortified defensive system some 16km (10 miles) deep, the myriad field fortifications of which were bristling with nearly 2500 machine-gun posts, some 480 prepared positions for assault guns, antitank guns and mortars, and mile upon mile of antitank ditches and wire entanglements sited principally on ridges lying across the path of the Allied advance. The Gothic Line would prove to be an extremely tough nut to crack.

Nevertheless, the perimeter of the shrinking Reich was becoming increasingly frayed. In the German homeland, the Allied strategic bombing campaign

Above: Red Army infantry aboard a T-34, the mainstay of Soviet armoured divisions from 1941 and the best all-round tank of World War II. From 1943 onwards the Red Army began its inexorable advance towards Germany.

was squeezing Hitler's war industry and the beleaguered populations of Germany's industrial cities. From the summer of 1944, RAF Bomber Command had been flying regularly by daylight. On 27 August 1944, 216 Handley Page Halifax heavy bombers of 4 Group, and 14 de Havilland Mosquitos and 13 Avro Lancasters of 8 Group, raided the Meerbeck oil refinery in the first major daylight raid mounted by Bomber Command since 12 August 1941, when 54 Bristol Blenheims had bombed power stations near Cologne. On the outward flight, escort was provided by nine squadrons of Supermarine Spitfires and the withdrawal was covered by a further seven squadrons. The bombers did not fly in tight formation like the Liberators and Flying Fortresses of the US 8th Air Force, but in loose 'gaggles'. There was intense flak over Meerbeck, but even so, there were no Allied losses. Production at the Meerbeck plant was not resumed until that October.

Bomber Command was fast moving towards a peak wartime strength with an average daily availability of 1600 aircraft, of which approximately 1100 were four-engined Avro Lancasters. The cream of Britain's scientific establishment had been absorbed in the development of the advanced technology employed in the strategic bombing offensive, while

the industrial resources devoted to the production of heavy bombers was, at a conservative estimate, equal to that which was allotted to the production of equipment for the British Army.

By night, Bomber Command's target-marking techniques had reached new levels of sophistication. In the summer of 1944, 5 Group developed the system of 'offset' marking, in which each aircraft of the Main Force approached the aiming point – already illuminated by flares and incendiaries dropped by bombers of the Pathfinder Force – on one of several pre-instructed headings. Although the Main Force bombers aimed for the same single marking point, the different angles of approach and timed overshoots provided several aiming points for the price of one successful marking attack by the Pathfinders.

Over Königsberg on 29 August 1944, there were three approach lines. In the attack on Bremerhaven on 18 September there were five, a method perfectly adapted to bombing a port stretching for 13km (8 miles) along the eastern shore of the Weser estuary.

Above: A formation of US 8th Air Force B-17 Flying Fortress bombers release their bombs through heavy cloud on the German port of Emden in October 1943. At this stage in the war, the Allied combined strategic bombing offensive was beginning to tell on German industrial output.

The Bremerhaven raid was carried out by 200 aircraft, which dropped 863 tons of bombs, including 420,000 thermite incendiaries. Photo-reconnaissance indicated that of a total built-up area of 152 hectares (375 acres) by 120 hectares (297 acres) had been destroyed. The techniques used at Bremerhaven were further refined in a raid which was conducted on Darmstadt on 11 September.

After the target had been marked by 627 Squadron's Mosquitos, 234 heavy 'bombers approached the aiming point – an old army-parade ground 1.6km (1 mile) west of the city centre – along seven lines of approach at varying heights and with each aircraft timing its overshoot by between 3 and 12 seconds. This ensured that the destruction was spread in an unfolding V-shape across the city. The Germans called it the 'Death Fan'. Destruction in the centre of Darmstadt was 78 per cent, and 70,000 of the city's 115,000-strong population was made homeless. In the Old City, only five buildings

remained standing. Some 8500 people perished in the 45-minute raid, about 90 per cent of them from asphyxiation or burning. A similar technique was used in the attack on Brunswick on 14 October. A firestorm was started in an area of the city that contained six giant bunkers and air-raid shelters housing more than 20,000 people. However, these people were saved by a 'water alley' driven through the blazing streets by high-pressure hoses and screened on each side by overlapping jets of water.

That the city had suffered such terrible damage led the Brunswick authorities to estimate that at least 1000 bombers must have carried out the bombing. Within 40 minutes over one-third of the population of 200,000 had been made homeless and nearly half the built-up areas of the city had been laid waste. In fact, this monumental attack had been carried out by only 234 aircraft. The chief of RAF Bomber Command, Air Chief Marshal Sir Arthur Harris, now believed that he had Germany by the throat. But despite the rain of destruction, the bombers had failed to deliver a knock-out blow to the Germans. The morale of Germany's civilians had survived the battering, in the same way that Londoners had weathered the Blitz in 1940.

Nor had German war industry been taken out of the equation. Under the managerial genius of Armaments Minister Albert Speer, overall industrial output had risen throughout 1944. In September the Reich's aircraft plants produced 3000 fighters. The same month, another wartime peak was reached as a total of 1854 armoured fighting vehicles rolled off the Reich's production lines.

Impressive though it was, this achievement masked the remorseless erosion of Germany's industrial base. The heavy components of the armoured vehicles' were fed into the pipeline months before in order to meet the long lead-times required in the manufacture of such weaponry. But as 1944 drew to a close, Allied bombing of the Ruhr had reduced pig-iron, crude steel and rolling-mill production to about one-third of the levels of January 1944. The effect was immediately felt in areas of production with short lead-times. The output of trucks, previously boosted by the rebuilding of all the disabled army trucks in Germany, fell away rapidly. During the first 10 months of 1944, the Army Ordnance Directorate had accepted 45,917 trucks, though truck losses in the same period were 117,719.

In addition to this was a growing fuel crisis. The production of aviation and motor gasoline was dipping, and ammunition output was also entering a downward curve. In September 1944, the German armed forces were firing some 71,100 tones (70,000 tons) of explosives, while production amounted to only half that figure. Nevertheless, the German railway and canal systems remained largely viable, and at the beginning of September, Speer informed the Führer, somewhat optimistically, that Germany's war stocks could be expected to last through 1945.

In 1944, Albert Speer had achieved a kind of miracle, principally with a policy of dispersal, and it is perhaps ironic that by dictating the terms on which German war industry should be organized, the Allied bombing offensive had made it more efficient. But dispersal bred its own problems. Economy of scale was sacrificed and greater demands were placed on badly stretched skilled-labour resources. Moreover, increased dispersal brought with it a greater risk of interruption of the production flow by the bombing of communications, and indeed this was to be the case in the winter of 1944/45. By February 1945, in the aftermath of the Ardennes offensive, the number of rail wagons available to the *Reichsbahn* (German railway system) had fallen from 136,000 to 28,000, about 10,000 fewer than were needed to sustain 25 per cent of industrial production. As the railway system collapsed, the heavy weapons which had been produced in the last surge of German war output lay stranded in their factory yards.

Above: An Avro Lancaster releases a 1814kg (4000lb) 'cookie' and a shower of incendiaries on Duisberg, a city in the heart of Germany's industrial powerhouse, the Ruhr. By autumn 1944, RAF Bomber Command had an average daily availability of 1600 aircraft.

Thus the late summer of 1944 saw the paradoxical situation in which Hitler's optimism, fed by his military and civilian advisers and the aides around him, convinced the Führer that Germany still possessed the material means to launch and maintain one last great offensive against the Allies ranged against the Reich. Conversely, the miscalculation of the Western Allies as to the destruction wrought by their day- and night-bombers contributed greatly to the belief – shared by Allied commanders and their intelligence chiefs – that Germany no longer possessed the muscle to deliver a mighty blow. As will be seen, there were some voices in Allied intelligence who adopted a more cautious view of German capabilities and intentions, but these voices did not carry the day.

Hitler believed that the matériel was at hand to fulfil his ambitions, but what of the manpower? The imminent disintegration of Germany's industrial infrastructure was to be paralleled by the haemorrhaging of her military manpower. In 1944, some 196 divisions had been destroyed, 3 more than had been mobilized in 1939. In the summer and autumn of 1944, total irrecoverable losses on all fronts were 1.46 million men, of whom some 900,000 had been lost on the Eastern Front alone.

At the beginning of October, German strength in the East stood at 1.8 million men, of whom about 150,000 were 'Hiwis' (*Hillsfreiwillige*), or voluntary aid); they were Russian volunteers who were given line-of-communications duties. This represented a drop of 700,000 on the figure for January 1944, a time when troops in the Western theatre could still be used as a reserve. These sobering figures should have given Hitler pause for thought. Instead they drove him deeper into the military fantasy world that had become his natural habitat. In December 1944, he told General Thomale: 'There is no foreseeable end to reorganization. Everything is in a process of flux – our national production, the state of training, the competence of commanders. But this is nothing new in history. Only just now I was reading through a volume of letters of Frederick the Great. This is what he writes in one of them, in the fifth year of the Seven Years' War: "There was a time when I went on campaign with the most magnificent army in Europe.

Below: The blackened hulk of Cologne cathedral rises above the devastated city. On 30/31 May 1942, Cologne was the target for Bomber Command's first '1000 bomber raid', a harbinger of the destruction Allied bombers were to visit on Germany's cities by the end of 1944.

Now I have a heap of rubbish – I possess no more commanders, my generals are incapable, my officers are no longer proper leaders, and my troops are of appalling quality." You can't imagine a more damning indictment, and yet this man has stuck it out through the war.'

Hitler never lost the chance to compare himself to Frederick the Great, but his method of dealing with the manpower crisis flew in the face of military good sense. Since the spring of 1943, the high rate of casualties on the Eastern Front, and the lack of reserves, had made it impossible to bring depleted divisions up to strength. In September 1944, the German ground forces numbered 327 divisions and brigades, of which 31 divisions and 13 brigades were armoured. But many of these existed only on paper. Logic dictated that divisions should be merged to maintain a sustainable ratio between combat troops and those in the auxiliary tail; this would have encouraged economical use of experienced officers,

Left: Albert Speer, Hitler's Armaments Minister and a brilliant technocrat, confers with the Führer at the latter's headquarters in the Wolfschanze (Wolf's Lair) in East Prussia. Speer could take much of the credit for sustaining German industrial output in 1944.

As the German Army burned away at its core, increasingly desperate measures were introduced. Conscription was extended to bring in 16- and 50-year-olds. Military hospitals were trawled for convalescing soldiers who were strong enough to hold rifles; they were drafted into the sardonically-named 'stomach' and 'ear' battalions, which were made up entirely of men who were suffering either from stomach complaints or defective hearing.

All the while, Hitler was juggling with numbers, reducing infantry divisions to six battalions, authorizing the formation of artillery corps with brigade strength and transforming regiments into divisions. In November, he agreed to allow Hiwis to fight in the front line, a decision which led to the creation of the Russian Army of Liberation, led by General Andrei Vlasov, who had been captured near Sebastopol in May 1942 when commanding the Soviet 2nd Shock Army. Vlasov did not receive the first division of his army until 10 February 1945, at which time it still lacked half of its clothing and equipment and virtually all of its motor vehicles.

The summer of 1944 saw the introduction, under the direction of *Reichsführer-SS* Heinrich Himmler, of the *Volksgrenadier* divisions, the name emphasizing their links with the German people rather than the *Wehrmacht* (German armed forces) hierarchy that Hitler had come to loathe and distrust. The *Volksgrenadier* divisions were scraped together from replacement units, badly mauled divisions and depot staffs. Each approximately 6000 strong, they were of limited military value, despite Himmler's assertion that their close links with the *Waffen-SS*, with Nazi Party ideology and with the people counted for more than military professionalism.

Addressing *Volksgrenadier* officers on 26 July 1944, Himmler left them under no illusion as to the rigours of the Eastern Front, where life expectancy for a company commander was no more than three months. A battalion commander could expect to survive for only four months before being killed or wounded. Nevertheless, Himmler concluded: 'So long as the Aryan lives, so long as our blood, Nordic-German blood lives, so long there will be order on this globe of the Lord God. And this task, from eternity out into the eternity of our *Volk* [people], is placed in the hands of each generation, especially ours. And when you see these periods of time, timeless, then I believe that each of you in the hour of difficulty and danger will realize what a short

NCOs (non-commissioned officers) and specialists, and the more effective use of motor vehicles, equipment and horses. Hitler's obsession with numbers frustrated any such rationalization.

The Führer insisted on replacing each of his lost divisions with the new ones. For Hitler, what mattered most was the number of divisions in the order of battle, not their strength or quality. Of this *rage de nombre*, Albert Speer gloomily observed: 'New divisions were formed in great numbers, equipped with new weapons and sent to the front without any experience of training, while at the same time the good, battle-hardened units bled to death because they were given no replacement weapons or personnel.'

The new formations Hitler willed into existence – in July to August 1944 no fewer than 18 divisions, 10 panzer brigades and nearly 100 separate infantry battalions – did no more than paper over the cracks. But this was just the beginning: a further 25 new divisions, some 1000 artillery pieces and a score of general headquarters brigades of various types were summoned up for October and November.

Above: The wrecked Bielefeld viaduct in Germany three days after it had been toppled by Bomber Command with 9979kg (22,000lb) 'Grand Slam' bombs. The Allied bombing campaign had crippled Germany's transport infrastructure by late 1944.

second that is in the life of the earth, in the life our *Volk*. And during this short second the only thing that matters is that he who lives precisely there (at that time) now does his duty …'

An approach much more practical than this gush of gibberish was adopted by Josef Goebbels, Hitler's propaganda minister. Hitler had belatedly proclaimed Total War on 13 January 1943, as defeat engulfed German 6th Army at Stalingrad. But over a year later, with disaster staring the Führer in the face, Germany had not undergone a total mobilization. In August 1944, Josef Goebbels was appointed Plenipotentiary for Total War and set to work with a will, scouring all the nooks and crannies of the Third Reich for any available manpower.

Women of 50 were drafted into war factories, where they worked a 60-hour week, to release men for the *Volksgrenadier* divisions. Former beauticians

and *U-bahn* (underground railway) ticket collectors were conscripted. This alone would not have sustained German war industry, which survived from crisis to crisis because of the 12 million foreign workers, including prisoners of war, in the Reich. The great majority were forced labourers impressed from occupied Europe from the beginning of 1942. Forced labour made up about 40 per cent of the German workforce, and in some war factories the proportion was as high as 90 per cent. They became breeding grounds for sabotage against Germany's war efforts as the war drew to a close.

A mood of weary cynicism gripped the German civilian population in the autumn of 1944. Recalling Hermann Göring's confident pre-war assertion that his fighters would sweep enemy intruders from the skies, Germans sarcastically referred to the Allied bomber streams penetrating the heart of the Reich seemingly almost without challenge as '*Parteitag Fluge*' (demonstration flights at the Nazi Party rallies at Nuremberg). However, one man did not share the general feeling of war weariness with the population of Germany, and that man was Adolf Hitler.

Adolf Hitler had fought the greater part of the war from the *Führerhauptquartier* (headquarters) at Rastenburg deep in the dense, dripping Gorlitz forests of East Prussia. Here in the *Wolfschanze* (Wolf's Lair), behind the barbed wire and minefields that surrounded Security Zone One, Hitler retreated into self-imposed isolation, moving in an airless world of maps and military conferences. From December 1941 he had assumed personal control of army operations, having dismissed the commander-in-chief, Field Marshal Walther von Brauchitsch.

Freezing in winter, stiflingly hot in summer, the Wolf's Lair fed off the Führer's enervation and gloom. Count Ciano, Benito Mussolini's Foreign Minister, found the atmosphere at Rastenburg an intensely depressing experience: 'One does not see a single colourful spot, not a single lively touch. The anterooms are full of people smoking, eating and chatting. Smell of kitchens, uniforms, heavy boots.'

Those who came and went, waited and smoked, or stood awkwardly silent as Hitler shuffled through the compound with his German Shepherd bitch Blondi at his side, were mere extras in a drama whose last act was being written by a man moving step by step away from reality. After the debacle at Stalingrad, Hitler strove to conceal his growing depression and deteriorating health behind a mask of rigid self-control. But the mask kept slipping, and his physical appearance shocked those on his staff who had not seen him for some time.

Visiting Hitler at his Ukraine headquarters, Vinnitsa, on 20 February 1943, to confirm his own appointment as Inspector-General of Armoured Troops, General Heinz Guderian found the Führer greatly changed since their last meeting which took place in December 1941: 'His left hand trembled, his back was bent, his gaze was fixed, his eyes protruded but lacked their former lustre, his cheeks were flecked with red. He was more excitable, easily lost his composure, and was prone to angry outbursts and ill-considered decisions.'

The *Feldherr* ('Great Captain') of the early years of the war had become a trembling valetudinarian, increasingly reliant on the quack remedies fed to him by his personal physician Dr Theodor Morell, who was dubbed the 'Reich Injection Master' by the Führer's entourage. But there were others who worked in the stifling confines of the Rastenburg complex who had even more drastic remedies in mind, remedies which involved the death of Hitler.

Right: Hitler takes a wintry walk with Albert Speer at Rastenburg. As the war went on, the Wolfschanze *increasingly became a prison for the Führer, whose isolation from the front line and the impact of the war on Germany's population staved off the shadow of impending defeat.*

One of them was Colonel Count Claus von Stauffenberg, an officer of the General Staff who had served with distinction in Poland, France and North Africa. Stauffenberg was severely wounded by a low-level strafing attack in April 1943, losing his right eye, right arm and part of his left hand. On his release from hospital, he joined the conspiracy to assassinate Hitler. This was given the codename 'Valkyrie', which was also the name given to a contingency plan which was to be activated in the event of a rising by slave labour in Germany.

Stauffenberg's duties included attending briefings at Rastenburg. Since the nature of his injuries apparently placed him above suspicion, his briefcase was never examined by the guards at the *Wolfschanze*. On 20 July 1944, Stauffenberg used this combination of circumstances to plant a bomb that he hoped would be detonated to kill Hitler.

By the end of June 1944, the relatively airy above-ground huts and bunkers in which Hitler had held

Above: German manpower shortages are reflected in this teenage intake into the Luftwaffe. *Conscription had been extended to those as young as 16 and as old as 50, but even so, by the winter of 1944, Germany's armed forces were desperate for replacements to fill their depleted ranks.*

his daily conferences had been replaced by concrete blockhouses and bombproof underground steel-and-concrete shelters with walls 6m (20ft) thick. On 20 July, the concrete bunker in which Hitler usually held his conferences was being repaired. The conference therefore took place in a flimsy hut above ground, and this saved Hitler's life.

When Hitler had taken his place, and the midday conference had begun, Stauffenberg laid his briefcase against the leg at the far right end of the heavy table on which the situation maps were being examined and made an excuse to slip out of the room. As he crossed the outer compound, he heard the bomb detonate. Stauffenberg boarded an aircraft bound for Berlin to announce the death of Hitler and the formation of a new government.

The announcement was fatally premature. During the conference, another officer inadvertently pushed the bomb away from its intended target behind a heavy wooden plinth supporting the table. When the bomb detonated, the force of the explosion blew out the top of the end of the table. Of the seven men standing at that end, four died and two more were gravely injured. The flash set light to Hitler's hair and clothing, shredding his trousers and burning his right

leg. The flimsy ceiling collapsed, bringing with it part of a roof beam which skinned Hitler's buttocks 'like a baboon's', as he later described it.

The shock of the assassination attempt and his seemingly miraculous survival gave Hitler an immense adrenalin boost. Bathed, and with his burns dressed and his right arm in a sling, the Führer donned a new uniform and drove to meet the arriving Benito Mussolini. Film footage of the event shows Hitler in manic high spirits on the platform of Rastenburg's secret railway station, codenamed 'Gorlitz', greeting a subdued Mussolini.

Hitler took Mussolini back to the ruined hut, gleefully giving a blow-by-blow account of his recent good fortune: the windows had been open at the time the bomb detonated, lessening the effects of the blast. Had he held the conference in a deep shelter, he would not have survived. Hitler told Mussolini that he had been saved by the hand of Providence and that he believed 'the great destiny which I serve will transcend its present perils and that all will be brought to a triumphant conclusion'.

The bomb plotters had failed. Failure at Rastenburg has been matched by a failure of nerve in Berlin. Vital hours were lost through vacillation,

Right: A young girl gives a drink to a member of the Hitler Jugend *(Hitler Youth) who was drafted in to man an antiaircraft battery in one of Germany's cities. Flak batteries were a threat to Allied bombers in 1944; in August 1944 US 8th Air Force lost 131 aircraft to them.*

poor organization and sheer bad luck. At 18:45 hours, the news of the Führer's survival was broadcast throughout the Reich and the conspiracy then collapsed. Only in Paris was a measure of success achieved, albeit temporary. General Karl-Heinrich von Stulpnagel, the Military Governor of Occupied France, succeeded in rounding up the SS and Gestapo, but without the backing of his commander, Field Marshal Gunther von Kluge. Aware that Hitler had survived, he was forced to release his prisoners.

The gallant Stauffenberg was shot that night in Berlin, the first in a grisly succession of executions. The conspirators, as well as those suspected of being sympathetic to them, were either given the dubious privilege of committing suicide or were executed after show trials. At least 250, including two field marshals and 16 generals, are known to have met their end in this way, the death agonies of some of them being filmed for the entertainment of the Führer and his entourage. In the fall-out of the failed

Above: Hitler seen at the Wolfschanze *(Wolf's Lair), his command post at Rastenburg, East Prussia, with the Italian Foreign Minister Count Ciano in the autumn of 1941. From 1941–44, Hitler spent much of his time at the* Wolfschanze.

Bomb Plot, an estimated 10,000 people were sent to concentration camps, gassed, shot or hung.

This bloodletting – a brutal echo of the 1934 'Night of the Long Knives' – seemed only to galvanize Hitler. His patience with the army, for long a dwindling asset, was now exhausted. His first recourse was to the spirit of National Socialism. General Fritz Fromm, executed after the Bomb Plot, was succeeded by Heinrich Himmler as head of the *Ersatzheer* (Replacement Army), whose task it was to provide not only replacements for the *Feldheer* (Field Army) formations but also to form additional field units to be committed to battle. The appointment of the hated *Reichsführer-SS* was greeted by the officer corps – by whom he was universally loathed – without a murmur of protest. Indeed, the hapless von Brauchitsch was wheeled out, willingly or otherwise, to condemn the traitors of July and laud Himmler's appointment as a sign of closer cooperation between the army and the SS.

Left: Clearing the rubble in Berlin in 1944. The absence of any able-bodied men serving in the armed forces meant that the responsibility for clearing the wreckage fell mainly on the shoulders of civilian women. During and after the war, they were dubbed 'rubble ladies'.

On 23 July, the new Chief of the General Staff, General Heinz Guderian, issued an Order of the Day in which he described the bomb plot conspirators as 'a few officers, some of them on the retired list, who had lost courage and, out of cowardice and weakness, preferred the road to disgrace to the only road open to an honest soldier – the road of duty and honour'. The loyalty of a unified army was then pledged to the Führer.

The next day it was announced that the service salute had been replaced by the 'Führer salute', with outstretched arm, and was to be mandatory for all *Wehrmacht* (German armed forces) personnel. If anyone needed reminding, Hermann Göring roused himself from his monumental torpor to observe that the salute was a 'special indication of the unshakeable loyalty to the Führer and of the close bonds of comradeship between the *Wehrmacht* and the Party'.

On 29 July, Guderian, prodded by Hitler, issued a new order designed to embed National Socialism deep in the philosophy of the army: 'Every General

Below: The Führer greets a visitor to the Wolfschanze *in early July 1944. On the far left is the tall figure of Colonel Count von Stauffenberg, who attempted to assassinate Hitler on 20 July. For his part in the plot, Stauffenberg was executed that same night in Berlin.*

Staff officer must be a National Socialist officer-leader, that is, not only by his knowledge of tactics and strategy but also by his model attitude to political questions and by actively cooperating in the political indoctrination of younger commanders in accordance with the tenets of the Führer'.

In the latter part of July 1944, revenge against those who had planned to assassinate him was one of the two major driving forces in Hitler's life. The second preoccupation was that of inflicting a major blow on the Allied lodgement in France. On the face of it, revenge seemed within the still formidable coercive power of the Nazi state. Inflicting a blow on the Allies seemed well nigh impossible.

In July, the Allies had fought a costly slugging match in Normandy. East of Caen, in Operation 'Goodwood'. General Bernard Montgomery, commander of ground forces in the Normandy invasion (Operation 'Overlord'), had launched a series of limited attacks intended to suck much of the German defensive strength into his sector. 'Goodwood' began on 18 July, involving all three British armoured divisions in Normandy – the Guards, 7th and 11th – in a battle of attrition that cost nearly 200 tanks to a dogged German defence.

It had been a chastening experience. When 'Goodwood' finally sputtered out on 20 July, it was 43 days after D-Day. The 'phase lines' drawn on the planners' maps before 'Overlord' had forecast that the Allies should be halfway to the Loire by that date. Nevertheless, 'Goodwood' had succeeded in pulling German Army Group B's armour back towards the British front at the moment when it had been concentrating on countering growing evidence of a gathering and powerful American offensive.

In July the Americans had been fighting a gruelling battle in the bocage country south of the Cotentin Peninsula. Between 18 and 20 July, the 29th and 35th Divisions had lost respectively 2000 and 3000 men in the battle for St Lô, five times the number of casualties suffered by the British armoured divisions in the same period east of Caen. However, these were outstripped by German losses. The Americans' principal opponent, 352nd Division, which had defended Omaha Beach on D-Day, had effectively ceased to exist after the battle for St Lô. Since 6 June the number of casualties suffered by German 7th Army had reached 116,000, for which only 10,000 replacements had come from the *Ersatzheer* (reserves). Matériel losses had been equally grave: to set against German tank production of 2313 in May to July, there had been losses of 1760 vehicles, one-third of them in the fighting in Normandy. To make it worse, only 17 replacements had arrived at the front in northern France.

Above: The wreckage in the conference hut in Rastenburg after Stauffenberg's bomb had exploded. Hitler's life was primarily saved by the flimsy construction of the building whose open windows dissipated much of the blast. As a result he sustained only superficial injuries.

Below: A visibly relieved Hitler takes the visiting Benito Mussolini on a tour of the conference hut at the Wolfschanze *shortly after the explosion of Stauffenberg's bomb. His survival convinced Hitler that he had been spared in order to fulfil his historic mission.*

On the morning of 25 July, four American infantry and two armoured divisions of General Omar Bradley's 1st Army attacked 7th Army between St Lô and the coast. Bursting through the front, they passed General George S. Patton's 3rd Army into the hinterland and the entrance to Brittany.

The main blow fell on von Choltitz's LXXXIV Corps, near Avranches. Field Marshal Gunther von Kluge, who had replaced Field Marshal von Rundstedt as Commander-in-Chief West and was on a whirlwind tour of the front, visited the headquarters of 7th Army on 30 July where, he wrote, he found the 'set-up farcical, a complete mess, the whole army putting up a poor show'. The chief of staff and von Choltitz were dismissed, but not the army's tough commander, SS General Paul Hausser, a hard-bitten veteran of the Eastern Front.

For some experienced German commanders, the game seemed to be up. Many would have agreed with Rundstedt's outburst at a staff conference; when asked what he would do, he barked, 'Make peace, you fools!' Rundstedt was removed from his post on 2 July, replaced by the more combative Kluge.

Below: The aftermath of the Bomb Plot. The trial before the People's Court in Berlin of Count General von Witzleben, former Commander-in-Chief West. An estimated 10,000 poeple were sent to concentration camps as a result of the Bomb Plot.

In the military and moral penumbra of Rastenburg, Hitler took a different view. Unlike Rundstedt, he had no choice but to fight on. By the end of July, the Führer had concluded that the final decision would be made in the West. On 31 July he subjected General Alfried Jodl, Chief of Staff of the *Oberkommando der Wehrmacht* (OKW – High Command of the German Armed Forces), to a long harangue about the need to make a concerted effort in the West, if need be at the expense of other fronts. The main thrust of the Führer's argument was that he would be in sole charge of the planning and command of the operation, which he would exercise from a headquarters yet to be chosen, possibly in the Black Forest or the Vosges. Hitler added that the Commander-in-Chief West was not to be informed of this decision. Jodl was to put together a small operational staff to provide Hitler with the information he required. In this meeting can be seen the genesis of the plan that was to become, in its final form, Hitler's offensive in the Ardennes.

The reasoning behind Hitler's decision can be simply stated. Throughout the war he had been concerned with the protection of the Ruhr, the heart of German war industry. Until June 1944, the threat to the Ruhr's factories had been posed by Allied bombers. But now, with the Front collapsing in the West, Allied ground forces were an approaching

menace. The lost mineral and industrial sources in Eastern Europe had been written off, but the Ruhr needed to be safeguarded at all costs. The Allied breakout in Normandy was gathering force, and would seem to be a greater danger than the convulsions in the East, where the Red Army had reached as far as Brest-Litovsk and was now readying itself for a concerted drive on Warsaw.

The classic dilemma of Germany's military history had been the resolution of the problem posed by fighting a war on two fronts, in the West and the East. Such great minds as von Moltke and Schlieffen had striven to avoid falling into this potentially fatal strategic trap. Hitler had tumbled in, and was now clawing his way out. The war in the East had forced Hitler to confront several unpalatable truths. The Soviet Union was too vast a territory in which to gain a decisive victory against the Red Army, whose capacity for renewal now seemed unlimited. After the terrible defeat at Kursk in July 1943, the story on the Eastern Front had been one of continuous Russian advance followed by German retreat.

Above: An ammunition truck is hit by German mortar fire in heavy fighting in Normandy during Operation 'Goodwood', the costly British attempt to draw in the German reserves in order to help an Allied breakout elsewhere.

Guderian later reflected on the aftermath of Kursk: 'There were to be no more periods of quiet on the Eastern Front. From now on the enemy was in undisputed possession of the initiative.'

To Hitler, the Soviet Union appeared to be a monolith, which was embodied by the huge, dominating figure of his fellow-dictator Stalin. Yet he had always retained a sneaking regard for Stalin. After all, they were both members of the same small club: the society of absolute dictators. In his table talk, Hitler would often reflect admiringly on the ruthlessness of Stalin. However, there was one very important difference between the two men. Both had arrived at a system of command which suited their particular temperaments, but while Hitler's solution left him in a state of uncreative tension with his generals, Stalin was eventually able to make the best possible use of the outstanding military professionals. These were men who had emerged since June 1941 and in the wake of Stalin's paranoid purge and were men who operated effectively but did not undermine Stalin's total authority over the Soviet Union's armed forces.

Unlike Hitler, who was a fatal combination of the dilettante and doctrinaire, imposing his own blueprint for every operation, Stalin tended to collect the opinions of those who mattered most, weigh up the pros and cons while applying his detailed knowledge of the overall situation, and then reach a decision. Usually he sanctioned a course of action on which STAVKA (the highest organ of field direction in the armed forces of the Soviet Union) had already been deliberating. Thus the view of the majority became Stalin views, encouraging the collective initiative of his commanders and enabling individuals to advance radical ideas for discussion. They were still his creatures, of course, there for the making and breaking, and crucial figures like Marshal Zhukov, his chief field commander, and Marshal Vasilevsky, his indispensable Chief of Staff, were under no illusion, knowing that they held their considerable powers only at Stalin's pleasure.

Below: The C-in-C West, Field Marshal Gerd Von Rundstedt, and staff officers inspect the Atlantic Wall in the spring of 1944. Rundstedt was removed from his post in July 1944 and reinstated in September. He had a jaundiced view of 'Autumn Mist's chances of success.

If Hitler saw the Soviet Union as a monolith, he regarded the grand alliance against Germany as potentially fractious and vulnerable. On 12 December, only four days before the Ardennes offensive was launched, he took his generals on a *tour d'horizon* of his strategic thinking as it had developed between the late summer and winter of 1944. He began by castigating the Allies:

'In the whole of history, there has never been such a coalition which consisted of such heterogeneous elements with such diametrically opposed objectives as the present hostile coalition against us. Ultra-capitalist states on the one hand, an ultra-Marxist state on the other. On the one side a dying world empire, that of Great Britain, and on the other a 'colony', the United States, anxious to take over the inheritance. The United States is determined to take Britain's place in the world. The Soviet Union is anxious to lay hands on the Balkans, the Dardanelles, Persia and the Persian Gulf. Britain is anxious to keep her ill-gotten gains and to make herself strong in the Mediterranean. These states are already at loggerheads and their antagonisms are growing visibly from hour to hour. If Germany can deal a few heavy blows, the artificially united front will collapse at any moment with a tremendous thunderclap. In the last resort wars end when one side or the other realizes that victory is impossible.'

The speech represented a distillation of Hitler's grand strategy as it had evolved from the beginning of August 1944. In the East the distances were too great, and the Red Army was too numerous to secure a decisive victory. In the West, however, there were no such tyrannies of space. But despite this difference, initially it proved impossible to stabilize the Front in the West and to launch a crippling blow against the Western Allies.

Below: A T-34 silhouetted by a blazing Russian village in the Kursk salient, July 1943. After Kursk, one of the decisive battles of World War II, the Germans were increasingly desperate in their attempts to hold back the ever-improving Red Army's advance.

CHAPTER TWO

The Crumbling Front

*Until the middle of October the enemy
could have broken through at any point he liked
with ease and would have been able to thrust deep
into Germany almost unhindered.*

General Siegfried Westphal

One casualty of the Falaise battle had been Field Marshal Gunther von Kluge, who had replaced von Rundstedt as Commander-in-Chief West in July. On 15 August, while he was on the front line near Avranches, his wireless tender was knocked out, cutting off communications with his headquarters for several hours. At Rastenburg, where Kluge was already a marked man – suspected of complicity in the Bomb Plot against Hitler – it was assumed that he was attempting to negotiate some kind of settlement with the Allies. On 17 August he was relieved of his command and received the dreaded order to return to Berlin. Kluge chose suicide.

On the day of Kluge's death, the German front in France was fast disintegrating as the Americans and British raced to close the pincers on the Falaise pocket. At the *Wolfschanze* (Wolf's Lair) General Heinz Guderian survived a bruising encounter with Hitler. He had been briefing the Führer on the state of the German armoured forces in the West and had observed that: 'The bravery of the panzer troops is not enough to make up for the failure of the other two services – the air force and the navy.' Hitler instantly flew into a towering rage and ordered Guderian to follow him into another room, where he

continued to berate his chief of staff in no uncertain terms. About this argument Guderian later was to observe: 'Our voices must have grown louder and louder, for eventually an adjutant, Major von Amsberg, entered with the remark, "The gentlemen are talking so loudly that every word is clearly audible outside. May I close the window?"'

The quick-thinking Major was able to defuse a nasty situation, but neither Hitler nor Guderian could stabilize the front in France. However, the speed of the German collapse had opened up a potentially serious rift over strategy within the Allied camp. Four Allied armies were straining at the leash: the Canadian 1st and British 2nd, which made up 21st Army Group, commanded by General Sir Bernard Montgomery; and the US 1st and 3rd Armies, which comprised the newly formed 12th Army Group, commanded by General Omar Bradley.

Allied Supreme Commander Eisenhower – who on 1 September had assumed control of Allied land forces from Montgomery (who was consoled by his promotion to Field Marshal) – favoured an advance into Germany on all fronts. This was a strategy which would enable Patton, on his right flank, to maintain his drive to the River Saar and which would also allow Montgomery to seize the vital Channel supply ports and overrun Germany's V-1 flying bomb and V-2 rocket sites on the left flank. Montgomery and Patton begged to differ. Both had their eyes fixed firmly on the Rhine.

Left: Field Marshal Gunther von Kluge, who succeeded von Rundstedt as C-in-C West in July 1944 but was relieved of his command a month later, suspected of being involved in the July Bomb Plot. Field Marshal Kluge committed suicide rather than return to be tried in Berlin.

Above: A road in the Falaise pocket in the summer of 1944, littered with the hulks of burnt-out vehicles and the bodies of German soldiers. At this stage the Allied High Command was confident that the German Army was finished as an effective fighting force.

Eisenhower's subordinates were two prima donnas, a contrast in opposites, who had to be managed with the greatest tact by the patient Supreme Commander. Montgomery was prim, teetotal and schoolmasterly, a stringy, birdlike man urging the men under his command to 'hit the enemy for six'. Patton was not given to breezy cricketing metaphors. He was the embodiment of all-American aggression who sported an ivory-handled Colt .45 in his holster and was a man firmly of the belief that you grabbed the enemy by the nose 'the better to kick him in the pants'.

Both men heartily loathed each other, the legacy of their race to Messina in the campaign for Sicily from July to August 1943. But this odd couple had more in common with each other than they would have cared to admit. They were both instinctive showmen – Patton's revolver was matched by Montgomery's eclectic array of cap badges – who concealed complex characters under a display of egotism. They prompted mixed emotions in the men they commanded, some of them less than complimentary. Patton's nickname in 3rd Army, 'Old Blood and Guts', was said to stand for 'Our blood, his guts.' Montgomery and Patton were the two most combustible elements in the Allied coalition.

Patton's 3rd Army had driven the enemy over the Meuse, which he had crossed at Verdun and Commercy at the end of August, having captured two bridges before the Germans could blow them up. Patton was convinced that he could slice through the forces he had been pursuing to 'bounce'

the Rhine in the area of Worms. On 21 August he wrote in his diary: 'We have at this time the greatest chance to win the war ever presented. If they will let me move with three corps ... we can be in Germany in ten days. There are plenty of roads and railways to support the operations. It can be done with three armoured and six infantry divisions ... It is such a sure thing that I fear these blind moles don't see it.'

The German High Command, however, was only too well aware of the growing peril. On 4 September Rundstedt had been reinstated as Commander-in-Chief West. According to his chief of staff, General Siegfried Westphal: 'The overall situation in the West was serious in the extreme. A heavy defeat anywhere along the front, which was so full of gaps it did not deserve the name, might lead to a catastrophe if the enemy were to exploit his opportunity. A particular source of danger was that not a single bridge across the Rhine had been prepared for demolition, an omission which took weeks to repair ... Until the middle of October the enemy could have broken through at any point he liked, with ease, and would have been able to thrust deep into Germany almost unhindered.'

Along the entire front on 7 September the *Westheer* could scrape together only 100 serviceable tanks. South of the Ardennes, 2nd Panzer Division fielded just three tanks. In contrast, Eisenhower could call on nearly 6000 medium and 1700 light tanks. At the beginning of September, of the 48 German infantry divisions in the West, only 13 were considered fit for offensive operations, 12 were partially fit and 14 were considered practically useless. Stretched along a 650km (400-mile) front, this amounted to an effective strength of little more than 25 divisions. *Luftwaffe Kommando West*, the successor to *Luftflotte 3*, which had flown in the Battle of

Above: A studied exercise in Allied solidarity. On the left, Patton with pearl-handled revolver, Bradley dressing down in the centre and an unusually jovial Montgomery on the right, sporting his customary eclectic array of cap badges on his beret.

Britain, could put up about 570 aircraft. Allied air strength in Britain and France stood at 14,000 aircraft, nearly 9000 of them American.

It was against this background that, on 16 September, Hitler presided over another crucial meeting at the *Wolfschanze*. Emerging from his quarters for the daily briefing, he presented a shocking sight to officers who had not seen him for some time. The keeper of the Führer's official diary, Major Percy Schramm, noted during the meeting that 'Hitler had suddenly grown old, his complexion looked unhealthy, he often stared vacantly, his back was bent, and his shoulders sunken, as if an invisible weight was crushing him. The most frightening impression, however, resulted from the tremble in his hands, which had become more pronounced in the last few months.'

For this, Hitler had Dr Morell to thank, rather than the effects of the Bomb Plot. The charlatan Morell had been treating the Führer for stomach cramps with large quantities of one of his patent medicines containing strychnine and belladonna. Hitler was gobbling so many of these pills that he was poisoning himself. However, despite the dreadful spectacle he presented, Hitler had a surprise in store.

The briefing passed without incident. But when it broke up, Hitler called for a smaller special meeting. Present were the Führer, General Jodl, General Wilhelm Keitel, Chief of the *Oberkommando der Wehrmacht* (OKW – High Command of the German Armed Forces), General Guderian and General Kreipe, representing the *Luftwaffe* and standing in for the absent Hermann Göring. Kreipe kept a detailed record of the meeting in his diary notes, although this was in violation of Hitler's express instruction that no notes of daily conferences should be retained, beyond the official transcript which was prepared by his own stenographic staff.

Jodl opened the briefing. In his low, measured voice and adroit turn of speech – calculated not to trigger a temper tantrum from Hitler – Jodl reviewed the relative strengths of the opposing forces in the West: 96 Allied divisions at or near the Front, and 55 German divisions. He added that an estimated 10 Allied divisions were en route from Britain to the

29

battle zone. Allied airborne units were still in England; some of them would appear the next day at Arnhem and Nijmegen.

Jodl then went on to address the problems of supply and the shortage of tanks, heavy weapons and ammunition. Next he turned to the situation in southwest France, where US VI Corps and the French II Corps had driven north from the 'Anvil' landings to Dijon and Besançon. He was cut short by Hitler. The Führer said: 'I have just come to a momentous decision. I shall go over to the counter-attack.' Jabbing his finger at the map on the table before him, he continued, 'Here, out of the Ardennes, with the objective – Antwerp!'

In the ensuing stunned silence, the Führer warmed to his theme. A strong German attack group, stiffened by some of the new *Volksgrenadier* divisions, would break through the Ardennes sector, which was thinly held by the Americans, and seize the Meuse crossings to take the Belgian port of Antwerp, which had been occupied by the British on 4 September. The drive to Antwerp would inflict 'another Dunkirk' on the British, in the same way driving them into the sea.

Below: Germany's 'map generals'. Hitler with Field Marshal Wilhelm Keitel (centre), chief of OKW, and General Alfried Jodl, the OKW Chief of Staff. Jodl was intimately involved in planning the Ardennes offensive, while Keitel's role was restricted to the amassing of fuel.

Hitler considered that Germany would need a maximum of two months to ready the offensive while German forces held their positions 'under any condition' on a line from the Swiss border to the Schelde estuary on the North Sea in Holland. Although Hitler did not allude directly to it, the last measure was clearly intended to deny the Allies much-needed supplies shipped to Antwerp from 95km (60 miles) upstream. The holding forces on the long German front in the West could expect no reinforcement; indeed, some panzer units from the Eastern Front would have to be transferred to the Ardennes sector for the attack. At this point, Guderian's protests were brushed aside.

Jodl also had a query. A German counteroffensive would be compromised by Allied air superiority. Hitler replied airily that the *Luftwaffe* would supply 1500 new aircraft to cover the attack. Even Kreipe ventured that this was a target beyond the reach of the enfeebled German air force. Hitler would have none of it, adding that the Ardennes operation would be launched at a time of year when mist and low cloud would ground Allied aircraft.

Jodl then made another point. German intelligence had indicated the strong possibility of an Allied airborne operation in Holland. Would this not disrupt Hitler's plan? The Führer ploughed on, the *Feldherr* once more and the master of events. The operation would be commanded by Field Marshal von Rundstedt. His restoration and reputation would boost the German Army's morale. In the coming weeks, the utmost secrecy would be observed. The meeting broke up. The die had been cast.

Adolf Hitler may have drifted into the realm of strategic fantasy in the middle of September 1944, but, despite his deteriorating physical condition, he retained a keen grasp of the logistical overstretch caused by the speed and scale of the Allied advance following the Normandy breakout. At the beginning of the month he had assured the reinstated Rundstedt that the Allies would soon outrun their supplies and their attenuated spearheads could be cut off with local counterattacks.

The Allied Supreme Commander, General Eisenhower, was constrained not only by the need to balance the competing claims of the commanders strung out along his 'broad front'. This strategy was also shaped by the supply problems caused by the Allied dash across northern Europe. Montgomery had urged on Eisenhower a plan for a massive 40-division drive across northern Germany, a mirror image of the German Schlieffen Plan of 1914. But political imperatives meant that Montgomery could never be given absolute priority at all times over Eisenhower's American subordinates. Moreover one

Above: Hitler, holding his arm and showing signs of strain after the Bomb Plot, accompanied by (left to right) Keitel, Hermann Göring and Martin Bormann. Keitel was dubbed 'Lakaitel' (little servant). Hitler thought he had 'the brains of a cinema commissionaire'.

Below: The Allied Supreme Command before D-Day. Eisenhower (centre) confers with Montgomery, while Bradley looks on from the left of the back row. On the right of the back row is Lieutenant-General Walter Bedell Smith, Eisenhower's indispensable chief of staff.

of them, Patton, was so far ahead of his planned objectives and timetable that, having left the Supreme Headquarters Allied Expeditionary Force (SHAEF) planners far behind, he was relying on a Michelin road map for directions.

The Allies had arrived at a point which, when planning the invasion, they had not expected to reach until May 1945. Supply was now the factor which dictated the Supreme Commander's options in the allocation of resources. The Allied air campaign in the months preceding D-Day had been so successful in destroying the French rail system that when the Allies broke out of their bridgehead the means to sustain their advance could be provided only by road, and this was not enough to meet the daily US divisional requirement of 700 tonnes of ammunition, equipment and rations. Eisenhower later would observe: 'The life blood of supply was running perilously thin through the forward extremities of the Army.'

Below: German troops march into captivity in France while an American tank rumbles past, raising dust as the Allies raced for Paris. German casualties in the battle for Normandy were 240,000 men killed or wounded. The Allies also took some 210,000 prisoners.

Eisenhower could only maintain the Allied momentum by giving scant resources to one commander and withholding them from another. In this unforgiving equation, Patton was the immediate loser. With the Rhine a mere 110km (70 miles) away, and with 3rd Army cut back to a fraction of its fuel requirements, Eisenhower turned off the tap.

The fuel shortage was exacerbated by a confusion of competing options. An airborne invasion of Belgium had been planned but never executed, causing a week-long interruption of air supplies and the loss of 1.5 million tonnes of fuel, which would have been enough to 'bounce' the Rhine.

This might not have mattered had the Allies managed to capture the ports along the Channel coast, thus cutting the distance the trucks would have to travel to the Front. But following Hitler's orders, Army Group B had left garrisons to hold Le Havre, Boulogne, Calais, Dunkirk and the mouth of the River Schelde. Le Havre was captured on 12 September and Calais was captured at the end of the month, though Dunkirk held out to the end of the war. Even more critically, the defences of the Schelde estuary were still in German hands as the month of November began.

Above: American troops parade in front of the Arc de Triomphe in Paris in late summer 1944. The city had fallen to the Allies on 25 August. Four days later the last German troops slipped across the Seine. The Allies raced on to Brussels, which was liberated on 3 September.

Although Montgomery was to be the beneficiary of the fuel crisis, he had played a significant role in creating it. British XXX Corps, commanded by Lieutenant-General Sir Brian Horrocks, had seized part of the port of Antwerp with all its harbour facilities intact; however, Montgomery had his eyes fixed on the Rhine and had failed to push north over the Albert Canal to clear the northern bank of the Schelde estuary. This enabled German 15th Army, which had been shunted into a pocket on the southern bank of the Schelde, to pull back to Walcharen and Beveland on the northern bank, thus leaving a large and useful bridgehead behind it.

In a remarkable operation, concluded on 23 September, the Germans managed to ferry 86,000 men, 616 guns, 6200 vehicles and a similar number of horses across the estuary and into positions that denied the Allies the use of Antwerp, as well as presenting a threat to Montgomery's left flank as he prepared to race to the Rhine. Antwerp was not opened to Allied shipping until 29 November.

By 4 September, the day on which the Germans began ferrying 15th Army to Walcharen, Montgomery had finalized the plan that he believed would clinch the priority argument in his favour. In Operation 'Market Garden', three divisions of Allied 1st Airborne Army were to seize the bridges on the Eindhoven–Arnhem road, establishing a 96km (60 mile) corridor along which British 2nd Army would race to outflank the German West Wall, the fortified German defensive line (popularly known as the Siegfried Line) that ran along the Dutch and French borders from near München-Gladbach along to the Swiss border near Freiburg. In Montgomery's words, 'Market Garden' was to be merely the preliminary to the mounting of 'a really powerful and full-blooded thrust towards Berlin'.

Eisenhower gave the go-ahead for 'Market Garden' at a bad-tempered meeting in Brussels on 10 September, during which Montgomery was forced to apologize after demanding that priority meant absolute priority, even if it halted the Allied southern armies in their tracks. However, the concessions which Montgomery had wrung from the Supreme Commander – the allocation of 1st Airborne Army, fuel priority and control of US 1st Army on the right flank – reinforced Monty's conviction that the Supreme Commander had chosen the northern axis as the route into Germany. He had never come to terms with having to yield operational command of the land forces to Eisenhower, and by insisting on

Above: Allied landing craft off the island of Walcheren in the Schelde estuary. Heavily defended by German forces, the Schelde estuary held the key to Allied control of the strategic port of Antwerp, which was not opened to Allied shipping until 29 November 1944.

the primacy of the northern axis, to which all else was to be subordinated, Montgomery was actually seeking to regain control by other means.

'Market Garden' was launched on 17 September, the day after Hitler's announcement of his plan for the counteroffensive in the Ardennes. A week later it ended in failure. British 1st Airborne Division had suffered 1000 casualties and 6000 men had been taken prisoner; it had virtually ceased to exist. Even after 'Market Garden' had irretrievably broken down, Montgomery was highly economical with the truth in his dealings with Eisenhower. The Supreme Commander had to wait until 8 October when a situation report from 21st Army Group left him in no doubt that the chance of a breakthrough had vanished. 'Market Garden' had done nothing more than create an awkward salient, leaving the now acute problem of the opening of the Schelde estuary unresolved. A smarting Montgomery was brought into line by a telephone call from Eisenhower's chief of staff, Lieutenant-General Walter Bedell Smith, who threatened to cut off his supplies if he did not expedite the clearing of the Schelde estuary.

The Allied 'stop-go' strategy gave the German Army a crucial breathing space in which to exploit its phenomenal ability to recover and regroup. A scarecrow army of 135,000 cadets, line-of-communications troops and convalescents was tasked with rebuilding the West Wall, much of which had been stripped in 1943 to bolster the Atlantic Wall. Before the invasion of Normandy, the West Wall's most prominent feature had been a deep belt of concrete 'dragon's teeth' tank obstacles covered by pillboxes. Now the Wall was strengthened with deeply echeloned trench systems behind minefields and barbed wire. These static defences were the spine of an elaborate defensive belt that ran through villages, farmhouses and woods. In this belt, skilfully positioned and protected machine guns, mortars and artillery were ranged on key approaches and road junctions, and the 88mm (3.45in) guns of the dug-in MkVI Tiger German heavy tanks were sited to make the best possible use of terrain.

Reichsmarschall Hermann Göring revealed the existence of six parachute regiments and a further 10,000 men from redundant *Luftwaffe* aircrew and groundcrew. They became 1st Parachute Army, commanded by General Kurt Student, the mastermind behind the airborne seizure of Fort Eben Emael in 1940 and the battle for Crete in 1941, and were inserted along the line of the Albert Canal.

A similar transformation was taking place in Patton's sector, where 1st Army, under General Otto von Knobelsdorff, was renewing itself. At the end of August, one of its corps commanders had estimated that 1st Army consisted of no more than 9 battalions of infantry, 2 batteries of artillery and 10 tanks. By mid-September, this army had been reinforced by the arrival from Italy of 3rd and 15th Panzer Infantry Divisions, as well as the badly mauled 17th SS Panzer Infantry Division. These formations were joined by two *Volksgrenadier* divisions, and also several battalions of police.

With Montgomery now finally turning his attention to the clearing of the Scheldt, Eisenhower reverted to his earlier 'broad front' strategy. General Omar Bradley, the commander of 12th Army Group, was given two objectives: US 1st Army was ordered to clear the area around the ancient city of Aachen, and US 3rd Army was ordered to advance on the industrial region of the Saarland and then on to the Rhine. At the southern end of the Allied line, the newly created US 6th Army Group, which was under the command of General Jacob Devers, was to attack through the mountainous Vosges region and on towards the city of Strasbourg.

The encirclement of Aachen by US 1st Army began in September, and the city fell on 21 October. There had been three weeks of house-to-house fighting during which both sides had sustained heavy casualties. Aachen was the first German city to be taken by the Allies. General Clarence Hübner, the commander of 1st Division, attended mass in Aachen's great cathedral, where Charlemagne had been crowned Holy Roman Emperor in AD 800. Eisenhower paid a visit there and fell flat on his backside in the mud just as he was about to address the waiting troops. A BBC reporter, Robert Reid, described the incongruous, almost comical scene in The Holy Roman Emperor's cathedral:

'It was an eerie experience wandering through the historic old place. I walked through the cloisters. Three chickens fluttered through the shattered windows and began pecking the dirt in search of food. Two American doughboys, who'd just finished a meal of bread and cheese, threw them some crumbs … I haven't seen many towns like this before. But this is Germany. Late this afternoon I watched a group of German prisoners being led through the wreckage. They were silent, bent and sick-looking. Maybe they saw more in that terrible scene than the wreckage of Aachen. They were taking with them into captivity a preview of the wreckage of Hitler's Germany.'

Autumn had now set in, bringing with it mist and driving rain which turned the ground into a quagmire. It was the wettest autumn on record. The open country of northern France and Belgium lay behind the Allies, who were now confronted with a hostile landscape in which dense, gloomy woods gave way to ranges of steep hills defended by an enemy fighting on his own soil. Allied casualties were to mount

Below: A German assault gun masked by an Allied parachute at Arnhem, September 1944. The failure of Operation 'Market Garden' was the final blow to Montgomery's hopes of playing the prime role in the defeat of German ground forces in northwest Europe.

steadily not only from enemy action, but also increasingly from trench foot and influenza as well as simple physical exhaustion.

With Aachen in American hands, the US 1st Army pushed northeast up the Stolberg Corridor, a narrow strip of open country which was hemmed in on the left by a straggle of industrial suburbs, and on the right by the glowering, dark mass of the Hürtgen Forest. This area was 130 square kilometres (50 square miles) of dense pine forests which were cut with steep gorges and packed with pillboxes and mines. In the next three months, the Hürtgen was to consume five US infantry divisions.

The Hürtgen had not been fully cleared in February 1945 when 82nd Airborne Division, commanded by General James M. Gavin, arrived to finish the job. Gavin found it incomprehensible that 1st Army's commander, General Courtney Hodges, had attempted to steamroller his way through the Hürtgen when on his southern flank there was a perfectly good approach road for tanks which bypassed the valley that had claimed so many American lives.

Below: A MkVI Tiger E heavy tank mounting an L/56 88mm (3.46in) gun. These tanks equipped heavy tank battalions of a panzer corps. Some 1350 were built before production ceased in August 1944. Principal drawbacks of the tank were its weight and bulk.

Right: A map showing the disposition of both sides after the failure of Operation 'Market Garden' and the Allied breakthrough of the Siegfried Line. However Allied progress slowed once they set foot on German soil, the Germans' defence suddenly stiffening.

Hodges had simply multiplied the combat effectiveness of the one German division in the forest and nullified the huge superiority he enjoyed in armour and air support. When Gavin asked a corps staff officer 'why in the world' Hodges had attacked through the Hürtgen, he was told most definitely that this was a 'no-no' question.

A 'no-no' question for Adolf Hitler in the autumn of 1944 was that of 'unconditional surrender'. Germany's war potential had been so drastically reduced that, even to allies like Japan, it was clear that Germany could no longer win the war. It seems that, late in 1943, Hitler sounded out the Allies as to the precise terms they had demanded at Casablanca in January of that year. Nevertheless, Allied insistence upon those terms before and after the July Bomb Plot effectively ruled out the possibility of ending the war by negotiation. Nor was it in Hitler's nature to admit the possibility of defeat.

Having ruled out capitulation, Hitler could only fight on in the hope or expectation that Allied dissension or miscalculation would hand him the

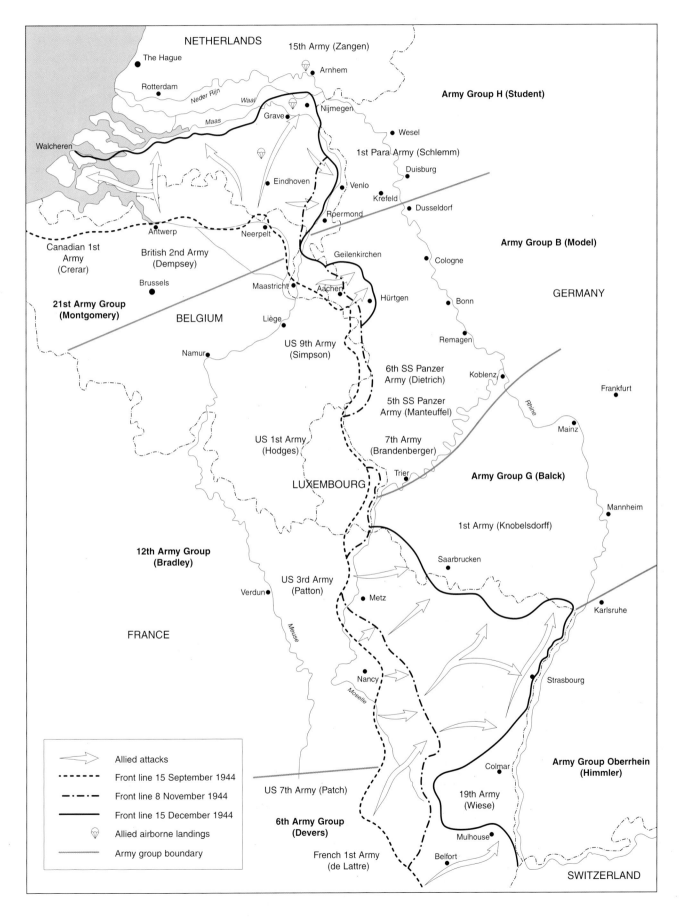

NETHERLANDS

15th Army (Zangen)

The Hague

Rotterdam

Neder Rijn

Waal

Maas

Arnhem

Army Group H (Student)

Walcheren

Grave

Nijmegen

Wesel

1st Para Army (Schlemm)

Eindhoven

Venlo

Duisburg

Krefeld

Dusseldorf

Roermond

Antwerp

Neerpelt

Geilenkirchen

Army Group B (Model)

Canadian 1st
Army
(Crerar)

British 2nd Army
(Dempsey)

Maastricht

Aachen

Cologne

GERMANY

**21st Army Group
(Montgomery)**

Brussels

BELGIUM

Liège

Hürtgen

Bonn

US 9th Army
(Simpson)

Namur

Remagen

6th SS Panzer
Army (Dietrich)

Koblenz

Frankfurt

5th SS Panzer
Army (Manteuffel)

Rhine

Mainz

US 1st Army
(Hodges)

7th Army
(Brandenberger)

LUXEMBOURG

Trier

Army Group G (Balck)

Mannheim

1st Army (Knobelsdorff)

**12th Army Group
(Bradley)**

US 3rd Army
(Patton)

Verdun

Saarbrucken

Metz

Karlsruhe

FRANCE

Meuse

Nancy

Moselle

Strasbourg

**Army Group Oberrhein
(Himmler)**

US 7th Army (Patch)

Colmar

**6th Army Group
(Devers)**

19th Army
(Wiese)

French 1st Army
(de Lattre)

Mulhouse

Belfort

SWITZERLAND

Allied attacks

Front line 15 September 1944

Front line 8 November 1944

Front line 15 December 1944

Allied airborne landings

Army group boundary

chance to reverse the course of the war. Like Frederick the Great, the Führer would have to continue the struggle until 'one of our damned enemies gives up'. Only then could a peace be secured that would guarantee the future existence of the German people, and that of Adolf Hitler.

Another of the Führer's mentors was Karl Marie von Clausewitz, who had maintained that attack was the best form of defence. However, Hitler was a wayward disciple, constantly violating the Clausewitzian principle that successful defence demanded the preservation of strength, which in turn is possible only if space can be traded for time. Hitler was seldom prepared to do this, on either the Eastern or Western Fronts, and by 1944 was fast running out of both commodities.

Nevertheless, Hitler was impelled to act. In General Jodl's words, 'We could not hope to escape the evil fate hanging over us. By fighting, rather than

Left: A German Sturmgeschutz *(assault gun) in Aachen. An infantryman rushes past clutching a* Panzerfaust, *a hand-held, recoilless antitank weapon effective against the side-armour and rear of Allied tanks at ranges up to 91m (100yd), one of the most cost-efffective of the war.*

Above: American armour in action during the fighting for Aachen, the first German city to be taken by the Allies, on 21 October 1944, after three weeks of house-to-house fighting which left much of it in ruins. Its fall coincidentally effected the breach in the German Siegfried Line.

waiting, we might save something.' However, the original proposals submitted to Hitler in separate plans by his military and civilian advisers did not meet with the Führer's wholehearted approval. Part of this strategy for survival – advocated by Armaments Minister Albert Speer and Adolf Galland, head of the *Luftwaffe*'s fighter arm – envisaged a total civilian mobilization combined with a massive effort thrown behind Germany's jet aircraft programme which, after a gestation period of six years, was now beginning to bear fruit.

Rather than risk an immediate throw of the dice, Jodl and his deputy, General Horst von Buttlar-Brandenfels, proposed a wide-ranging series of measures, shifting the main effort to the West, which would be reinforced by large-scale withdrawals of troops from Scandinavia and Italy. The army would receive a huge injection of unemployed personnel from the *Luftwaffe* and the navy, and the entire

Above: German troops surrender to Americans in the autumn of 1944.
The German Army was able to draw on its capacity for renewal and
regeneration before the launching of the Ardennes offensive, but it was
the last occasion on which Hitler delivered a major blow to the Allies.

Below: Göring being briefed on the latest war situation. As the
Luftwaffe would be unable to contest the skies over the Ardennes with
the Allies, the decision to launch the offensive in the depths of winter
ensured that the weather would not be ideal for the Allied pilots.

Right: Hitler confers with Göring at the Berghof, his mountain retreat in the Obersalzberg, shortly after the Allied landings in Normandy in June 1944. By then the Luftwaffe's *fighter arm in France was a spent force, though great hopes were placed on its new jet aircraft.*

Replacement Army (some two million men) – including all training units – would be drafted into combat divisions. Finally, there would now be a mass mobilization of manpower, way beyond the measures which were introduced by Goebbels in the late summer of 1944, and Germany would become a fortress under martial law.

Hitler impatiently brushed these proposals aside. His disillusionment with Göring and the *Luftwaffe*, a wasting asset since 1942, did not encourage him to take heed of Speer and Galland. Nor did Jodl's latest proposal appeal to him. These measures would have to wait until February 1945, when the Red Army had steamrollered its way into the heart of the Third Reich. In order to meet the present threat, Hitler turned to a strategic compromise.

The Führer was determined to launch an offensive, but where was the blow to fall? In August the General Staff had prepared plans for offensive operations in the East, while the *Westheer* would fight a defensive battle with its back to the West Wall. This option was ruled out by the speed of the Allied advance through France and the Low Countries, and the sheer size of the Soviet threat. After the war, Jodl rationalized the situation. The attack had to be launched in the West 'because the Russians had so many troops that even if we had succeeded in destroying 30 divisions it would have made no difference. On the other hand, if we destroyed 30 divisions in the West, it would have amounted to more than one-third of the invasion army.' In fact the figure was nearer a half of the Allied force in Europe.

Hitler endorsed this view because of his low opinion of the morale of the British and Americans. He felt that the Americans in particular lacked the stomach for a fight: 'If we succeed we shall smash up half the enemy front and then we'll see what happens. I do not believe that in the long run the enemy will be able to stand up to the 45 divisions we will have available by that time.' The situation in the West would be stabilized, public opinion in America would force a US withdrawal from Europe, and Germany could then once again turn East: 'We shall master our fate all right.'

Once the theatre had been determined, the planning was turned over to the planners of the *Oberkommando der Wehrmacht* (OKW – High Command of the German Armed Forces). Hitler specified the five factors that were essential to success: German positions would have to resist all

Allied attempts at breakthrough without committing the forces assembled for the German breakthrough; tactical surprise must be achieved; a period of bad weather was absolutely essential in order to ensure that the Allied air force was grounded during the first 10 days of the offensive; the breakthrough must be exploited with the utmost speed; and other fronts, particularly the East, must be relatively quiet during the outset of the offensive.

Close examination of Allied strength and capabilities suggested that the enemy intended to close with the Rhine on a broad front north of Cologne, and at Metz, where the objective was the Saar Basin. The numerical ratio between the Allies and the German forces was approximately 2:1. Although the Allies were suffering ammunition shortages, the German planners considered that they were still capable of launching large-scale offensives. They discounted the possibility of an Allied amphibious landing in the Ems estuary and a repetition of airborne landings on the scale of Operation 'Market Garden'.

Five options emerged from these deliberations. Operation 'Holland' was a single-thrust attack to be launched from the bridgehead at Venlo with the objective Antwerp. Operation 'Liège–Aachen' was a double envelopment driving northwest through the Ardennes then turning north to link with a secondary attack launched simultaneously from the area northwest of Aachen with the aim of smashing up the Allied forces trapped in the resulting salient. Operation 'Luxembourg', a twin-pronged attack,

Below: German infantry. The soldier in the centre is leaning on a Sturmgewehr *assault rifle, gas-operated and largely made from steel pressings, but nevertheless a reliable and effective weapon. The assault rifle is now the standard infantry weapon in most of the world's armies.*

drove on Longvy from central Luxembourg and the Metz area. Operations 'Lorraine' and 'Alsace' envisaged envelopments with the objectives Nancy and Vesoul.

The choices were rapidly narrowed down to the first two options. Operation 'Holland' was persuasive but carried with it the greater risk. Operation 'Liège–Aachen', which later became known as the 'small solution', offered the greatest chance of success. Hitler's response was to combine the two options into a 'big solution', a bold stroke but one that left the offensive with two objectives to be gained with forces adequate only for one. Rundstedt, who was not informed of the plan until as late as 22 October, referred to Hitler's decision – with heavy irony – as 'almost' a stroke of genius.

The rationale behind the 'big solution' lay deep within the Führer's complicated, and often contradictory, thought processes. Antwerp offered a target the speedy capture of which – following a bold thrust – would confer a huge psychological boost on the Germans. It would also sunder the British in the north from their American allies to the south, thereby precipitating a fatal rupture in their alliance. Hitler also seems to have believed at this point that the Canadian component of Montgomery's 21st Army Group would simply give up, pack up their weapons, and go back home.

Above: The monocled Field Marshal Model, commander of Army Group B, visits a forward observation post of a Volksgrenadier *Division on 18 October 1944. A tough veteran of the Eastern Front, and tenacious in defence, Model committed suicide on 21 April 1945.*

Although he made few direct allusions to 1940 during the planning stage, it was in the Ardennes that Hitler had secured the vital breakthrough in the Battle of France. Once again, the apparent weakness of Allied dispositions in this sector invited a second bold stroke. Finally, the heavily wooded Eifel would provide suitable cover for the assembly of the breakthrough force. Hitler's military genius would wrest back the initiative from the Allies and decisively alter the course of the war. The cutting edge of the offensive would be provided by units withdrawn and rehabilitated from the debacle in France, and to this end, on 13 September, all the SS formations which had been fighting in France were withdrawn from the line for rest and replenishment.

Hitler decreed that the offensive's objective was to 'destroy the enemy forces north of the line Antwerp–Brussels–Luxembourg, thus to achieve a decisive turn of the Campaign in the West, and possibly of the entire war'. Rundstedt was ordered to break through the thinly held front of US 1st Army between Monschau and Wasserbilling with Army Group B, commanded by Field Marshal Walther Model, cross the Meuse between Liège and Dinant, seize Antwerp and the western bank of the Scheldt estuary and, in conjunction with this main attack, launch strong elements of the adjoining Army Group H in a supporting attack from the north.

The 53-year-old Model was a tough customer, famously foul-mouthed and never without a monocle. As Hitler's confidence in the older generation of generals had fallen, Model's star had risen and he had become the Führer's favourite 'fireman', particularly in Russia, where from 1942 he successively commanded 9th Army, and Army Groups North, South and Centre. In the East he had demonstrated that he was an excellent tactician, although stronger in defence than attack. After Rundstedt's dismissal, Model had temporarily been Commander-in-Chief West, that was, before Rundstedt's reinstatement to his old post. During the weeks leading up to the launching of the Ardennes offensive, and also in concert with Rundstedt, Model had tried, but despite all efforts had nonetheless failed in his attempts to convince Hitler to settle for the 'small solution' approach to the offensive in the West.

Below: The hard-drinking Hitler favourite Sepp Dietrich, whose 6th Panzer Army was tasked by the Führer with delivering the Schwerpunkt *(decisive blow) in the Ardennes. Hitler's faith in his old comrade was to prove misplaced and destructive to the entire operation.*

In the Ardennes offensive, Hitler intended Model's principal breakthrough instrument to be 6th Panzer Army, commanded by SS General Sepp Dietrich, which was to make a dash for the crossings of the Meuse on both sides of Liège, and of its tributary the Vesare. Setting up a strong defensive front in the eastward fortifications of Liège, 6th Panzer Army would then make for the Albert Canal between Maastricht and Antwerp, reaching the area to the north of Antwerp later. This would be achieved with 12 divisions, 4 of them armoured. Dietrich's command was designated a Panzer Army in 1945, but Hitler often referred to it as such in late 1944.

Sepp Dietrich was one of the 'old fighters' of the Nazi party. He had enlisted in 1911 at the age of 19 and in World War I had risen to the rank of Sergeant-Major. By 1918 he was in a tank battalion and, in the years immediately following Germany's defeat, had become involved with the fledgling Nazi Party. In 1928, Dietrich was given command of Hitler's bodyguard which, after the purge of the SA in the 'Night of the Long Knives' in 1934, became the *Leibstandarte* Adolf Hitler. Dietrich remained in command of this formation until it became the foremost unit of the *Waffen-SS*, fighting as a regiment in Poland, as a combat group in France in 1940, as a brigade in August 1940 and as a division for the invasion of Greece. It also fought in Russia between 1941 and 1942 and again between 1943 and 1944, before returning to Belgium.

During the summer of 1944, Dietrich commanded I SS Panzer Corps in northern France. His experiences in Normandy had left him a chastened man. On 7 June he was ordered to drive the Allies into the sea. But with only two divisions, he failed and, in the process, lost the greater part of his panzer corps. After the war, Dietrich observed that: 'There is only one person to blame for that stupid, impossible operation – that madman Adolf Hitler.'

In the autumn of 1944, however, Dietrich still remained one of Hitler's trusted generals, although Hitler's faith in the SS veteran's abilities as an army commander would eventually cost him dear. Göring considered that Dietrich had been over-promoted and at best was a competent divisional commander. Others were less generous, claiming that he should have remained in the rank of Sergeant-Major.

The task of covering 6th Panzer Army's left flank went to 5th Panzer Army, destroyed in Tunisia in May 1943 and reformed in Normandy in August 1944. It was to cross the Meuse between Amay (to the west of Liège) and Namur, and prevent Allied reserves from the west from attacking 6th Panzer Army along the Antwerp–Brussels–Dinant line. It comprised seven divisions, four of them armoured.

Its newly appointed commander was the diminutive, hard-driving General Hasso Eccard von Manteuffel, one of the German Army's leading experts on armoured warfare. He was involved in the early stages of Germany's armoured programme and at one stage had served as an instructor at the Panzer Troops School. Between 1940 and 1941 Manteuffel commanded a Motor Infantry Regiment in Erwin Rommel's 7th Panzer Division, first in France and then in Russia, rising to head a brigade before moving to Tunisia early in 1943 as a divisional commander. Back on the Eastern Front between 1943 and 1944, he led 7th Panzer Division and following that the crack *Grossdeutschland* Panzergrenadier Division, with whom he was often able to establish local superiority over his Russian enemy with manoeuvre and mobility, making the best use of ground cover. In the Battle of Targul Frumos, near Jassy in Romania, in May 1944, Manteuffel's 160 tanks (Tigers, Panthers and Mk IVs) shot up 350 of 500 attacking T-34s and IS-2 'Stalin' heavy tanks. Many of *Grossdeutschland*'s tanks were damaged, but only 10 were destroyed. Such engagements, Manteuffel concluded, demonstrated that 'in a tank battle, if you stand you are lost'.

In contrast to the roughneck Dietrich, Manteuffel was an aristocratic Prussian. As such he was a representative of the military caste that Hitler had come to despise. Nevertheless, Hitler was prepared to listen to this highly capable, undemonstrative officer who was not mesmerized by the Führer's mystique and who was more than able quietly to express his own point of view in meetings.

The third army selected for the Ardennes offensive was 7th Army, which had been virtually destroyed in the Normandy fighting and the long retreat from France. Now it was being rebuilt with new *Volksgrenadier* divisions and paratroops trained as infantry. Its commander was General Erich Brandenburger, an officer of no great flair but one who could be relied on to 'play everything by the book'. The role of 7th Army was twofold: to shield the southern and southwestern flank of the two panzer armies as they drove through the Ardennes and then on to Antwerp, and to establish defensive positions starting south of Dinant along the River Semois and ending astride Luxembourg. Brandenburger's advance was to be sufficiently forceful to gain the time and terrain to build up a strong defensive position to the rear; 7th Army was to field one armoured and seven infantry divisions.

A supporting attack was to be launched from the north by 15th Army, transferred from Army Group H to Army Group B. With three armoured and six infantry divisions, it was to mount holding attacks between Roermond and Eupen to tie down and then destroy Allied forces in that sector. Additionally, 15th Army was tasked with assuming control over those units of 6th Panzer Army committed to defensive positions along the River Vesdre after the mobile elements of 6th Panzer Army had crossed the Meuse. There was also a reserve of three armoured and four infantry divisions available. The offensive was codenamed *Wacht am Rhein* (Watch on the Rhine), a name that would confirm the Allied belief that Hitler was preparing a defensive battle which he hoped would deny the Allies the ability to conduct river crossings into the heart of the Reich.

In addition to these formations, the pack for the Ardennes offensive was to contain a joker. To ensure that 6th Panzer Army was able to secure the undestroyed crossings of the Meuse, Dietrich was given the services of 150th Panzer Brigade, which was commanded by SS Colonel Otto Skorzeny.

Below: Panzer General Hasso von Manteuffel, one of the German Army's leading experts in armoured warfare. The dynamic Manteuffel was 157cm (5ft 2in) tall; his friends dubbed him 'Kleiner' (Little One). He left his mark on the Ardennes offensive.

The 36-year-old Skorzeny – who, like Hitler, was an Austrian – had joined the *Waffen-SS* at the beginning of the war, and had won the Iron Cross in Russia before being invalided back to Germany. Having recovered, Skorzeny joined the SS's Section Six, a clandestine unit which specialized in sabotage and intelligence-gathering. This was to lead in July 1943 to a meeting with Hitler at Rastenburg. At the Wolf's Lair, Hitler tasked Skorzeny with the rescue of Benito Mussolini from a mountain hotel on Italy's Gran Sasso where he had been imprisoned by the Fascist Grand Council, which was seeking to make peace with the Allies. Hitler had made a good choice, and for his part Skorzeny fell completely under the spell of the Führer.

On 12 September, Skorzeny and a hand-picked team of commandos landed gliders in a mission to snatch Mussolini from his prison. This feat was accomplished without a shot being fired. Skorzeny, a tall, commanding figure, personally escorted Mussolini – now a crestfallen, shrunken figure – to his reunion with the Führer, and for his services was decorated and promoted. Thereafter Skorzeny became Hitler's favourite commando, and he was often used in daring operations, such as the successful kidnapping in September 1944 of the Hungarian dictator Admiral Miklos Horthy.

A month later Skorzeny was back at Rastenburg to be briefed for a new mission. To Skorzeny, Hitler seemed like a man transformed. The Führer launched into a dazzling *tour d'horizon* of the Western Front and the options prepared by the OKW for the counteroffensive against the British and Americans. When Hitler came to the Ardennes, he announced that he had reserved a vital mission for Skorzeny. Special units wearing British and American uniforms and riding in captured Allied tanks and other vehicles were to race ahead of the main force to the River Meuse, where they were to seize as many bridges as they could. In addition they were to create the maximum amount of confusion behind the Allied lines by giving false orders, cutting communications and lowering Allied morale by spreading wild stories of German success. Hitler gave the operation the codename 'Greif' (named after a mythical animal), promoted Skorzeny to Lieutenant-Colonel and awarded him the German Cross in Gold. Skorzeny was doubly honoured for it would seem that, in the run-up to the Ardennes offensive, he was the only man not to have been sworn to the strictest terms of secrecy by the Führer.

From the outset, however, Skorzeny was hampered by a signal lack of men and tools to do the job. He had been promised two companies of Shermans but had to make do with just two tanks, one of which broke down. Twelve Panthers were mocked up, none too convincingly, as Shermans. There was no shortage of American antitank guns and mortars but little ammunition. US battle dress was also in short supply. The fluent English-speakers he had been promised failed to arrive, and those potential 'Greif' commandos he had been sent came from such a wide variety of backgrounds that it would have taken months to weld them into a cohesive commando formation. Skorzeny was obliged to rely heavily on specialist units that had trained for earlier operations, and some paratroops. These men would form the core of Skorzeny's commandos. The reality of the 'Greif' operation was to fall far below the expectations which had been raised by the Führer in the mesmerizing pep talk he had given Skorzeny in the Wolf's Lair.

Right: The execution of one of Skorzeny's 'Greif' commandos, Private Manfred Pernass. Pernass was captured on 18 December 1944, two days into the Battle of the Bulge and, with his two companions, was executed as a spy. They died shouting 'Heil Hitler'.

CHAPTER THREE

The Battleground

It was obvious to me that the available forces were far too small —
in fact no soldier really believed that the aim of reaching Antwerp
was really practicable. But I knew by now it was useless to protest
to Hitler about the possibility of anything.

Field Marshal Gerd von Rundstedt

The hilly, forested Ardennes, held on a 145km (90-mile) front by only six American divisions, was considered a 'quiet' sector. Soldiers amused themselves by shooting wild boar from spotter aircraft. In the Ardennes, routines resembled those on similar sectors in World War I. By day men filled sandbags, strung wire and strengthened their foxholes. Officers hid their rank bars in order to avoid the attention of enemy snipers.

The nights were more dangerous, and filled with sudden, savage mortar and artillery bombardments and aggressive patrolling in search of prisoners for interrogation by intelligence officers. The flavour of life in the Ardennes in the early autumn 1944 was vividly captured in the diary of Staff Sergeant Henry Giles of 291st Combat Engineers, who was based at Steinfort in Luxembourg and was working on a bridge across the River Our for the US 4th Armored Division. On 1 October Giles wrote:

'Some of the wildest things can happen. I didn't have the Sgt of the Guard last night. Think Loftis did. Anyway it was set up and the security was posted. Then a work detail had to go out and repair a culvert. They either didn't know the password or had forgotten or something went snafu. Anyway

Left: A photograph taken during the battle for the Ardennes illustrates the type of terrain the offensive was fought over. Hilly and heavily wooded, it was far from ideal tank country, with narrow lanes proving to be congestion points for both Allies and Germans alike.

some kid got excited, thought they were Krauts and started shooting off his rifle. Today we heard practically the entire artillery of the 4th Armored was alerted ... And there's a weird story about one of the artillery crews. Seems like they got their own private dame. One of the boys swear it's the truth. Says she visits them every two or three days and they 'queue' up. Asked why he didn't join the line. He said, much astonished, 'Hell, them artillery boys'd murder you.' He's a sort of mild fellow, quiet type, doesn't talk much and just the way he said it sent us into convulsions.'

This was the Ardennes, which Petrarch had described six centuries earlier as 'the savage and inhospitable forests from which warriors and arms emerge at great risk'. In August 1914, General Lanzerac of the French 5th Army had warned the Army commander on his immediate right, de Langle de Cary, of the dangers that would confront his impending attack in the Ardennes: 'All this country is eminently suitable for the defensive and for ambushes ... you will not enter into this region, and if you do you will not return from it.' In the event, de Langle thrust in and suffered heavy losses.

Although the Ardennes was considered the graveyard of military ambition, and an unforgiving and inhospitable terrain, it had in fact witnessed many successful military operations. In the 20th century alone the Germans had successfully exploited the region twice, in 1914 and crucially earlier in World

War II in 1940. Nevertheless, in 1944 the legend of its impenetrability, especially in the depths of winter, exercised a powerful influence.

The Ardennes does not lack parts that present formidable barriers to a large army. On stretches of the Meuse, for example between Charleville and Givet, the approaches are protected from the east by beetling cliffs. At Dinant the only access to the river is through wooded, winding gorges, problematic terrain for tanks and easily blocked by determined demolition teams. But on the high plateau of the Ardennes the landscape lends itself to armoured operations; the forests are broken up by extensive clearings. The Arlon–Bastogne–Neufchateau triangle – in 1940 the main approach route of German 7th Division – is for the most part flat, open country.

The most dense forest and the most forbidding terrain of the Ardennes area lie close to the German frontier. In the north, the Hautes Fagnes ridge, a trackless moor where peat bogs alternate with forest, reaches the highest point in the region at nearly 915m (3000ft). To the southeast of Hautes Fagnes, dense forests run back to the road centre of St Vith. In September 1944, American troops had established positions 16km (10 miles) to the east of

Below: The American troops guarding the sector of front in the Ardennes were not of the highest quality. Sent there deliberately to rest or have their first taste of combat in a quiet part of the line, they were ill-prepared to meet the German attack.

St Vith, on the ridgeline of the Schnee Eifel, just inside the border of Germany, and a daunting obstacle to any attacker.

Several miles to the west of the Schnee Eifel is another high ridge, nicknamed 'Skyline Drive' by American troops familiar with the rugged landscape of the Shenadoah Mountains in Virginia. Behind Skyline Drive lies a gorge cut by the Clerve and Sure rivers. After absorbing the waters of the Clerve, the Sure drains southeastwards to the frontier with Germany, where it takes in the River Our and forms the border with Germany until it joins the River Moselle northeast of Luxembourg City at the southern end of the Ardennes.

Along the frontier the Ardennes offers only one corridor suitable for military movement, a sector some 8km (5 miles) wide, which starts at the northern end of the Schnee Eifel. It is known as the Losheim Gap, after the village of Losheim that lies just inside the German side of the frontier. 'Gap' is a relative term. Although the terrain is not thickly forested, a 3km (2-mile) belt of woodland bars the way to more open country inside Belgium, and the landscape alternates between steep hills and deep valleys. Nevertheless, as Rommel demonstrated in 1940, a bold commander could skilfully negotiate the trials of the perilous Losheim Gap.

The roadnet in the Ardennes was extensive, although much of it threaded a winding way through forests and valleys, and its passage through sharp

defiles or thick forests afforded defenders ample opportunity to cut or block an enemy's progress. In three years of occupation, the Germans had come to know the landscape, with all its advantages and drawbacks, in great detail. In autumn, the region's climate is wet and misty; in winter, snow often builds up in thick drifts. To the occupying Americans, the Ardennes seemed to offer limited military attraction and small strategic advantage to a Germany reeling on the ropes.

In the autumn of 1944, Supreme Allied Headquarters had deemed the Ardennes a secondary front, maintaining the bulk of American and British forces to the north and south. To the north, the end of October saw the recently arrived US 9th Army, commanded by General William H. Simpson, assume responsibility for the area from Aachen north to Roermond. In mid-November, Simpson committed his raw 84th Infantry Division in a joint operation with the British 43rd (Wessex) Division which was designed to punch out a salient jutting westwards around the town of Geilenkirchen.

The British and Americans fought their way through a maze of grimly defended positions in hilly country scarred with slagheaps and furnaces, and dotted with dreary industrial towns. When US 9th Army's offensive slithered to a halt in the snows of December, it had penetrated the West Wall to a depth of up to 16km (10 miles) at a cost of 1333 killed, 6864 wounded and 2059 missing. Thousands

Above: Behind the American front line in the Ardennes sector, a light armoured car squeezes past a caterpillar howitzer tractor. Icy, narrow roads made up much of the sector's roadnet and presented a formidable challenge to any attacking armoured force in winter 1944.

more had succumbed to pneumonia and trench foot, as well as to combat exhaustion.

Patton had also found the going tough to the south, in Lorraine, where he was faced by Army Group G, which was commanded by General Hermann Balck, a highly professional officer. Patton had declared that he would go through the West Wall 'like shit through a goose', but Balck made the most of the defensive possibilities which were offered by a succession of river lines – the Moselle, Meurthe and Seille – and the network of fortifications built in the region between 1870 and 1914. Conducting a skilfully handled withdrawal, Balck denied Patton the city of Metz until 13 December, when its surrounding fortresses were finally cleared.

In a private letter written to the US Secretary of State, Henry L. Simpson, Patton declared ironically: 'I hope that in the final settlement of the war you insist that the Germans retain Lorraine, because I can imagine no greater burden than to be the owner of this nasty country where it rains every day and where the whole wealth of the people consists in assorted manure piles.'

The Ardennes did not provoke such hostile emotions. The GIs stationed in the sector were able to

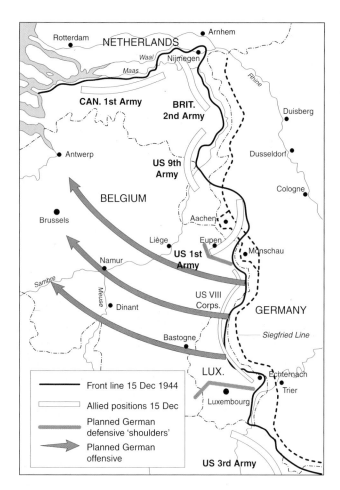

Front line 15 Dec 1944

Allied positions 15 Dec

Planned German defensive 'shoulders'

Planned German offensive

Left: The German plan of attack, with 6th Panzer Army in the north delivering the Schwerpunkt *and racing to Antwerp. Manteuffel's principal task was to cover Dietrich's left flank. Dietrich became bogged down; the main chance of German success passed to 5th Panzer Army.*

28th Division, which had lost 5000 men in two weeks of bloody fighting in the Hürtgen, occupied a 40km (25-mile) front on River Our running down to the junction of the Our and Sur.

From early October, 2nd Division had held a 29km (18-mile) front that took in the Schnee Eifel and continued almost to the Luxembourg border. To free 2nd Division for an attack on the Roer dams, 106th Division, with no combat experience, began moving into the line early in December. The commander of 2nd Division, Major-General Walter M. Robertson, had made repeated requests to reinforce the Losheim Gap, originally held only by a single cavalry reconnaissance squadron attached to 2nd Division. Finally, on 11 December, the headquarters of 14th Cavalry Group arrived to take control of that squadron and provide another one.

It speaks volumes of the low priority given to the Ardennes that such a critical sector was so sparsely defended. But in this part of the front the defence was spread very thin. The right flank of 99th Division, which lay next to the Gap, was protected by its only reserve infantry battalion. The 2nd Division placed one of its two reserve infantry battalions on its left flank close to the Gap. The only other indication of the recognition of the Gap's significance was provided by the decision of General Troy Middleton, commander of VIII Corps, to site eight of his XIII Corps artillery battalions in positions from which they could fire either into the Gap or into the sector that contained the Schnee Eifel. In the north of the Ardennes, covering Monschau, was 102nd Cavalry Group, a light force that fielded armoured cars, light tanks and a small number of self-propelled 75mm (2.95in) assault guns.

At the Supreme Allied Headquarters at the end of August, Major-General Kenneth Strong, Eisenhower's G-2 (chief intelligence officer), wrote: 'Two-and-a half months of bitter fighting, culminating for the Germans in a blood-bath big enough even for their extravagant tastes, have brought the end of the war in Europe within sight, almost within reach.' Eisenhower echoed this view two days later when he noted: 'The defeat of the German armies is complete, and the only thing now needed … is speed.'

But as the autumn set in, speed was not the *leitmotif* of the Allied advance. Nevertheless, Allied optimism remained undented by any fears of a massive German riposte, the very thing that Hitler was steadying himself to deliver. He refused to modify

enjoy a time out of war, periodically relaxing on a 48-hour pass at the army's dozen rest centres in Luxembourg and Belgium, where they could enjoy a shower, drink watered beer and see a film. United Service Organizations (USO) entertainers were occasional guests, some of them big names back home; the arrival of Marlene Dietrich in December was eagerly awaited. Beer and ice cream were available in the towns to the rear. On 15 December, Private Joe Schectman wrote his parents: 'We are billeted as comfortably and safely as we were in England. Of course, there's no telling how long I'll be in this paradise. But as long as I am, I'll be safe.'

The front line in the Ardennes was manned by battered or raw formations, a combination of old folk's home and nursery. By the second week in December, the southern end of the front was held by 4th Infantry Division, which had suffered 6000 casualties in the Hürtgen. Immediately to its north were units of the green 9th Armored Division, which was rotating armoured infantry battalions from one of its combat commands through a section of 28th Division's front. The battalion's tanks were kept some miles to the rear, and 9th Armored's two other combat commands further back. The experienced

Above: American troops with a mortar, feared by most infantrymen throughout the war. The US Army used 60mm (2.3in) and 81mm (3.1in) mortars with infantry and had a 107mm (4.2in) rifled mortar for chemical warfare companies as a heavy infantry support weapon.

the plan for 'Watch on the Rhine' along the lines suggested by von Rundstedt and Model, whose cautious protests were reinforced in November by von Manteuffel. All three were also worried about adequate petrol supplies for the offensive, a task that Hitler had delegated to the head of the *Oberkommando der Wehrmacht*, Field Marshal Wilhelm Keitel, a mere military cipher but an efficient quartermaster who succeeded in amassing the anticipated requirement of nearly 28 million litres (5 million gallons). Unfortunately, only half of this requirement would be on the west bank of the Rhine when the offensive actually began.

The only changes Hitler would discuss were those relating to timing and tactics. As for timing, the date originally set for the offensive had been 25 November, but this proved an impossible deadline. The date was pushed back to 10 December and, on 7 December, it was moved again, to the 14th. On tactics, Hitler was also flexible.

When he had first seen the Führer's orders for the offensive, Manteuffel was astonished by the fact that they laid down the method and timing of the opening attack. The artillery was to open fire at 07:30

hours and the infantry assault was to be launched at 11:00 hours. Between these hours the *Luftwaffe* was to bomb headquarters and communications. The armoured divisions were not to be brought into action until a deep penetration had been achieved by the infantry. The artillery was distributed over the entire frontage of the attack.

As Manteuffel later observed: 'This seemed to me foolish in several respects.' He immediately set to work on an alternative, which was approved by Model with the proviso that it was up to Manteuffel to argue it out in person with the Führer. Manteuffel insisted that Model accompany him, and the two of them met Hitler in Berlin on 2 December.

Manteuffel told Hitler that the opening bombardment would merely 'wake the Americans up'. They would then have three hours in which to react before the German assault was launched. Manteuffel went on to suggest, as diplomatically as possible,

Above: American GIs in poorly-dug defensive positions. The hard ground, often affected by frost, was very difficult to dig, and so these troops have been left exposed to any German artillery or mortar attack. A box of rations sits open behind the nearest trench.

that the infantry was not as good as in the earlier years of the war and was unlikely to make the deep penetration required by Hitler's plan in such difficult terrain. The American defences consisted of a chain of forward defence posts, with their main line of resistance well behind. This would be hard to pierce.

Manteuffel suggested several tactical changes. First, the attack should go in at 05:30 hours, under cover of darkness. This would limit targets for the artillery but would enable it to concentrate its fire on

key targets – batteries, ammunition dumps, head-quarters – the location of which was known. He then proposed the formation of a 'storm battalion' from each infantry division composed of the most experienced officers and men. These battalions were to advance at 05:30 hours in darkness without covering fire and pass around the Americans' forward defence posts, avoiding fighting until they had made a deep penetration, and lit by Flak unit searchlights projecting their beams on the clouds to bounce downwards, providing 'artificial moonlight'.

Hitler was urged to adopt this plan if the offensive was to have any reasonable chance of success. According to Manteuffel, Hitler accepted these suggestions without demur: 'It would seem that he was willing to listen to suggestions made to him by a few generals in whom he had faith – Model was another – but he had an instinctive distrust of most of the other senior generals, while his reliance on his own immediate staff was mingled with a realization that they lacked the experience of battle conditions ... At the same time their lack of fighting experience tended to make them underrate practical difficulties, and encourage Hitler to believe that things could be done that were quite impossible.'

There was to be one extra element in the composition of the force for *Herbstnebel* ('Autumn Mist'), as the Ardennes offensive was now called. After the collapse of the German Front in France and the Allied thrust into Belgium, Hitler had sent for General Kurt Student to form a fresh front in southern Holland. Student had been the presiding genius of German airborne operations in Scandinavia, Holland and Belgium in 1940, and Crete in 1941. Thereafter German paratroops had fought as infantry. Student was given command of a scratch force, 1st Parachute Army, which consisted of a number of depleted infantry divisions stiffened with a number of parachute units that were undergoing

training. The Parachute Army was to form part of Army Group H, alongside the newly formed 25th Army, which was commanded by Student.

On 8 December, Student was informed of the imminent offensive in the Ardennes and ordered to provide one parachute battalion, comprising 1000 men under Colonel Graf Friedrich August von der Heydte. The unit was attached to 6th Panzer Army and, after some confusion, was tasked with dropping on Mont Rigi near the Malmédy–Eupen–Verviers crossroads in order to create a flank block to delay Allied reinforcements coming from the north.

After Hitler's rejection of Rundstedt's proposal for a 'small solution', the latter had receded into the background, leaving it to Model and Manteuffel, who had more chance of influencing Hitler, to fight for technical changes to the plan. As Rundstedt observed: 'It was obvious to me that the available forces were far too small – in fact no soldier really

Below: General Student (in peaked cap) consulting a map during the landing on Crete in 1941. Hitler called on Student to lead Army Group H, consisting of a mix of infantry units and paratroops fresh from training.

believed that the aim of reaching Antwerp was really practicable. But I knew by now it was useless to protest to Hitler about the possibility of anything.'

Rundstedt was to play only a nominal role in the final conference, held on 11 December in his headquarters at Ziegenburg Castle, near Bad Nauheim, which was attended by Hitler, Model, Manteuffel and approximately half the corps and divisional commanders involved in 'Autumn Mist'.

Under the stern gaze of SS guards, they listened to a two-hour rant from the Führer on the absolute necessity for *Lebensraum* (living space), the glories of Frederick the Great, his own geopolitical triumphs of the 1930s and early war years, and the fatal cracks and contradictions in the alliance arrayed against him.

On the 12th, as Hitler briefed a second set of commanders, he announced his final concession. The jump-off date would be put back by 48 hours, to Saturday 16 December. Rundstedt's misgivings were echoed by the faithful Sepp Dietrich, who had been kept out of the picture until the last minute. He

Below: An Enigma machine, variations of which were used by all the branches of the German armed forces to transmit their messages in code. First reconstructed by the Poles, their research and Enigma machine copies were passed to the French and British in June 1939.

complained: 'All Hitler wants me to do is to cross a river, capture Brussels and then go on and take Antwerp. And all this in the worst time of year through the Ardennes when the snow is waist deep and there isn't room to deploy four tanks abreast let alone armoured divisions. When it doesn't get light till eight o'clock and it's dark again at four and with re-formed divisions made up chiefly of kids and sick old men – and at Christmas.'

One of the greatest Allied technological triumphs of World War II was the breaking of the German Enigma code by cryptoanalysts working at Bletchley Park, a Victorian country house some 100km (60 miles) from London. By 1944 the ability to read German messages encoded on the Enigma machine, in some cases in real time, exercised a powerful influence on Allied strategic and operational thinking. Codenamed 'Ultra', Enigma traffic covered a kaleidoscope of activity, from the movements of individual German officers across Europe to the thoughts of the Führer himself. Such was the faith placed in the security of Enigma that at no point in the war did German intelligence come close to the realization that the Allies had broken into the code that bound together so much of the German war effort: military, naval and industrial.

On 27 September, the Allied cryptoanalysts at Bletchley Park deciphered a message which had come from the operational headquarters of the *Waffen-SS*, dated 18 September, directing that all SS units on the Western Front be withdrawn from the line for rest or refitting, beginning with 1st, 2nd, 9th and 12th Panzer Divisions and 17th SS Panzergrenadier Division and three Tiger tank battalions as well as the headquarters troops of I SS Panzer Corps. All of these formations were to be assigned to the 'staff of 6th Panzer Army, the setting up of which has been ordered by *Obergruppenführer* (General) Sepp Dietrich'.

The deciphered message was relayed to Eisenhower's headquarters on the afternoon of 27 September and flowed down to all subordinate commands, including armies and tactical air commands. On 1 October, the Supreme Headquarters Allied Expeditionary Force (SHAEF) G-2, Major-General Strong, noted in his weekly intelligence summary that the Germans were withdrawing armour from the line in an apparent effort to provide a panzer reserve north of the Ardennes. At this stage, Strong made no reference to 6th Panzer Army.

Above: A German soldier in a foxhole late in 1944, waiting for the next Allied attack. As well as his Panzerfaust, *he has two automatic rifles, a formidable array of firepower. Such firepower helped the German armed forces counteract the Allied numerical superiority.*

Below: German paratroopers of Student's 1st Parachute Army, seen on the frontline in late 1944 wearing their distinctive helmets. They are manning an MG 42 machine gun. Since 1941 the paratroopers had been used only as conventional ground units.

Above: Field Marshal von Rundstedt and General Sepp Dietrich inspect the Atlantic Wall in the spring of 1944. During the Allied invasion of Normandy, Dietrich was commander of the I SS Panzer Corps. The two men were polar opposites.

'Ultra' decrypts continued to track further withdrawals throughout the month of October, and a stream of intercepts located divisional assembly areas east of the Rhine in Westphalia, or dealt with the problems attendant on releasing units from the line. It was also noted that SS Panzer divisions were to be brought up to full strength, and the withdrawal schedules were recorded. Yet another message indicated that Hitler had personally ordered the withdrawal and creation of 6th Panzer Army.

However, it was not until the end of the first week in November that Major-General Strong specifically named 6th Panzer Army, citing a German deserter as the source of his information. He also observed that 5th Panzer Army had left the line in Lorraine which – unknown to Strong – was the first move of General von Manteuffel's headquarters to the Aachen sector.

Allied intelligence then turned to consider what might be done with the SS divisions. Were they being readied for a counterattack or a spoiling

attack? While it was wrestling with this problem, another source of intelligence opened up. From early 1941 the United States had been reading Japanese diplomatic ciphers in a code-breaking operation known as 'Magic', the equivalent of Bletchley Park's 'Ultra' success. Allied intelligence now had an intercept of a report by Baron Oshima, the Japanese ambassador in Berlin, noting a meeting with Hitler in which the Führer had indicated that there would be a German offensive in the West after the beginning of November.

Early in November, Bletchley began tracking *Luftwaffe* movements to the West, commencing on 8 November with the transfer of units to airfields in Holland. A week later, a message emanating from the higher reaches of the *Luftwaffe* ordered daily reports on the serviceability of all aircraft. The sender used the word *Jägeraufmarch*, which Bletchley noted was a term for the assembly of forces for a planned operation. It had been used by German intelligence when pondering the disposition of Allied forces on the eve of D-Day. By 23 November, Bletchley concluded that the *Jägeraufmarch* was complete. Nobody at Bletchley, or SHAEF, saw any significance in these movements. With hindsight we can see that these intercepts reflect the *Luftwaffe*'s attempts to meet Hitler's initial deadline for 'Watch on the Rhine' at the end of November. Allied intelligence chose to interpret them either as a move to stiffen air defences against Allied bomber streams or as support for a German counterattack to blunt a new Allied drive to the Ruhr.

In early November, units of 6th Panzer Army began to transfer to the west bank of the Rhine. This, too, was noted, and General Strong concluded that the new panzer reserve was to be used against an Allied drive in the north. Other possibilities considered by Allied intelligence included a spoiling attack from positions northwest of Aachen to drive down both banks of the Meuse in a move similar to that urged by Rundstedt and Model in their 'small solution'. None of these scenarios made any reference to the Ardennes. By the third week in November, the consensus in Allied intelligence was that the probable mission of 6th Panzer Army was to counterattack an Allied crossing of the River Roer, probably in concert with 5th Panzer Army, whose arrival in the area of Aachen had been detected.

'Ultra' was also amassing a mounting pile of decrypts relating to troop movements linked with requests for air protection. A significant number of these requests were linked to railheads inside the Eifel. For example, on 3 December, in a request for protection, Army Group B named the ground units involved in these movements: among them was

326th *Volksgrenadier* Division at Gerolstein near the Schnee Eifel, and not far from Monschau, where the division actually attacked. On 7 December, Army Group B demanded the provision of fighter cover for almost the entire Schnee Eifel. None of the cover provided for both rail movements and railheads came from those airfields which had been recently reinforced with additional aircraft.

By now, teams at Bletchley had managed to break into the Enigma traffic of the *Reichsbahn* (the German railway system). A total of 800 trains had been earmarked to move the German attack forces into position for Operation 'Autumn Mist'. Bletchley Park picked up signals relating to at least half these movements, indicating a massive transfer of troops to the West. Simultaneously, reconnaissance and fighter pilots of 9th and 19th Tactical Air Commands were picking up movements which indicated a build-up in the Eifel. Night reconnaissance by the few available Northrop P-61 Black Widow night-fighters detected convoys with dimmed lights on many of the roads west of the Rhine. The Black Widows also detected possible troops assembly areas, which could be seen from the air as irregular patches of shielded lights, set away from the roads.

Above: A German 3.7cm (1.45in) Flak *gun mounted on a halftrack. During the build-up to 'Autumn Mist' the Germans provided their rail network with strong antiaircraft defences. Of much greater help was the predicted winter weather, which kept Allied fighter-bombers grounded.*

But the Allies had formed a picture – a German counterattack near Cologne – and paid little heed to intelligence that did not support this scenario. Thus intercepts of requests for aerial reconnaissance of the region around Eupen and Malmédy – which lay on the direct route to US supply dumps at Liège – went unheeded, as did requests for reconnaissance of the most direct route through St Vith and across the Ardennes. A message of 3 December was intercepted stating that the reconnaissance of the bridges across the Meuse was of 'the greatest urgency'. Another message, of 8 December, requested 'a good photo of the Maas [Meuse] crossings from Maastricht to Givet' to be given priority over other tasks.

Of course, traffic requesting reconnaissance in the Ardennes was outweighed by a factor of 3:1 by requests for reconnaissance around Aachen and aerial protection for trains unloading at Cologne. This was part of the German deception plan, aimed at drawing the Allied gaze north, away from the Ardennes.

Above: German troops encoding messages on an Enigma machine. To the war's end, the Germans remained convinced that the security of Enigma was uncompromised. In the build-up to the Battle of the Bulge, the Allies were not alerted by clues in Enigma traffic.

In the Ardennes sector itself, the commander of VIII Corps, General Middleton, was becoming increasingly concerned about the thinness of his front. Early in November he had been visited by Eisenhower and General Omar Bradley, commander of 12th Army Group, at his headquarters in Bastogne. Middleton was at pains to point out his weakness but was told that the Germans, like the Americans, seemed to be using the sector in order to rest battle-weary formations and also to give new formations some combat experience.

Not everyone was so sanguine. On 24 November, Patton would write in his diary: 'First Army is making a terrible mistake in leaving VIII Corps static, as it is highly probable that the Germans are building up east of them.' Patton had every right to be concerned because part of his line of advance took in the southern portion of the Eifel. Moreover, his own G-2, Colonel Oscar W. Koch, had been tracking German troop movements, presumably with the aid of 'Ultra'. On 9 December, Koch informed Patton that, by his own reckoning, in the German lines opposite VIII Corps were 4 *Volksgrenadier* divisions and 2 panzer divisions, with some 100 tanks in immediate reserve and 3 *Volksgrenadier* divisions nearby. Thus VIII Corps was facing a bigger concentration than the rest of 1st or 3rd Army. Koch's conclusion was that the Germans intended to move forces in the Eifel north or south to meet the Allied threat, and were using them to lure US divisions away from the main intended German attack by launching a diversionary offensive.

Patton was sufficiently impressed by Koch's argument to agree to 'limited planning' to counter any threat that might emerge from the Ardennes. But even so, this was not to interfere with 3rd Army's plans to launch a fresh offensive on 19 December.

At the headquarters of 1st Army, another intelligence officer was becoming worried. Colonel Benjamin A. 'Monk' Dickson was considered an overly alarmist intelligence man by his fellow officers. At times he listed formations in the German order of battle that were known to be elsewhere, these were dubbed 'Monk's shrubbery'. At the end of

November, troops of US 9th Army had captured an order issued on 30 October by German LXXXVI Corps which called on all units of the corps to screen for men with a knowledge of 'the English language and also American dialect' to volunteer for a 'special unit' the Führer had ordered to be raised 'for employment on reconnaissance and special tasks on the Western Front'. The order also directed 'captured US clothing, equipment, weapons and vehicles were to be collected "as equipment of the above troops" '.

This lapse in security revealed the existence of Otto Skorzeny's 'Greif' commandos. On 10 December, before he went on leave to Paris, Dickson issued a G-2 intelligence estimate that warned of a German counterattack between Roermond and Schleichen, to the north of the Ardennes. His trip to Paris was subsequently delayed by bad weather. At a staff meeting at 1st Army's headquarters in Spa, the Grand Hotel Britannique, Dickson declared, 'It's the Ardennes!' and jabbed frantically at the map on the table between Monschau and Echternach.

Below: General Troy Middleton (right) was commander of VIII Corps, stationed in front of the Ardennes. He raised his fears about the weakness of his position during a visit by Eisenhower and Bradley in November 1944, but was told not to worry.

Having slept on this dramatic hunch, Dickson issued a situation report during the following morning. In this report, however, he limited himself to the observation that it seemed as if the enemy would launch 'a limited scale offensive' in order to gain a morale-boosting Christmas victory. He then left shortly afterwards, bound for Paris.

Below: A German Flakvierling *antiaircraft gun mounted on the chassis of a MkIV Panzer, heavily camouflaged to prevent Allied aircraft from spotting its position. Although the* Luftwaffe *was little-feared by the end of 1944, Allied pilots had a healthy respect for German flak crews.*

There was another nervous intelligence officer at the headquarters of 12th Army Group in the Place de Metz, Luxembourg. Brigadier-General Edwin L. Sibert, General Bradley's G-2, had driven through the Ardennes with Bradley to visit Montgomery's headquarters in northern Belgium. Both men were struck by the absence of men and installations behind the front line and discussed the possibility of a German attack. Bradley said: 'When anyone attacks, he does it for one of two reasons. Either he is out to destroy the hostile forces or he's going after a terrain objective.' Bradley believed that neither

Above: German preparations for 'Autumn Mist' had to be carefully shielded from the Allied reconnaissance aircraft. Even the presence of a catering unit complete with field kitchen could have revealed the Germans' intentions to the Allies.

alternative could be obtained in the Ardennes, and if the Germans decided to attack there, it was unlikely that they would be able to make 'decisive progress' through such difficult country. If they came, the Americans would 'chew them up'.

This confident assertion did not prevent Sibert from fretting over an 'Ultra' intercept of a *Luftwaffe* order to reconnoitre crossings of the Meuse from Liège to Givet with aircraft to be forced through at low level if bad weather prevented high-level flying. Sibert despatched Colonel William H. Jackson to the SHAEF headquarters and then to London to liaise with British intelligence. He returned empty-handed.

Sibert was also prompted by his terrain expert, Major Ralph Ingersoll, to suggest to Bradley that a concentration was taking place in the Eifel. As a result, Bradley requested, and was refused, a reinforcement of one augmented division. There the matter rested, and Sibert himself concluded in a report of 12 December that Germany was on the point of collapse: 'With continuing Allied pressure in the south and the north, the breaking point may develop suddenly and without warning.'

At SHAEF headquarters, General Strong decided that the troop movements in the Eifel were just that: troops moving through to concentrate against Allied thrusts to the north and south. At a briefing – which was chaired by Lieutenant-General Walter Bedell Smith, Eisenhower's Chief of Staff – he indicated that the reserve panzer divisions had three possible uses, and these he listed in order of importance: they might be sent to reinforce the Eastern Front; they could counterattack an Allied penetration; or they could stage a relieving attack either through the Ardennes, or through Alsace.

The intelligence background to 'Autumn Mist' demonstrates the downside of the 'Ultra' triumph. By this stage in the war, Allied commanders expected the information it gleaned to be quite specific. Nor were they prepared to reconsider or modify the picture they had constructed of German capabilities and intentions. They anticipated that the enemy would helpfully conform to their own fixed view of the war and, as a result, had made an assumption likely to explode in their faces. It suited them to believe that Rundstedt, the most orthodox of professional soldiers, was running the show in the West, and the German armies in that theatre would be employed along sound military lines to counter Allied drives to the Rhine and Ruhr. Allied intelligence missed the vital point that the re-fitting SS divisions were to be an OKW reserve and thus entirely at the disposal of Hitler, not Rundstedt, who by this stage in the war ruefully reflected that the only troops he effectively commanded were the guards outside his door. As one historian of the Ardennes offensive has written of the Allied intelligence chiefs, 'They looked in the mirror for the enemy and saw there only the reflection of their own intentions.'

As the preparations for Operation 'Autumn Mist' moved forwards, wrapped in the tightest security and concealed by the mists of the early winter, the Allies turned to what they did best: arguing with each other. On 10 October, Montgomery renewed his campaign to be placed in charge of the land battle. In notably undiplomatic language, Montgomery

Below: German artillery knocked out on its way to the front. Nearly 2000 pieces of general support artillery were assembled for 'Autumn Mist' and 9 new artillery units known as Volksartillerie *corps, each equipped with up to 100 pieces, plus 7* Volkswerfer *rocket brigades.*

bluntly made the suggestion that Eisenhower was out of touch with the front, and that it was clear that the American had been increasingly inclined to fall back on hazy political compromise.

Eisenhower replied with a letter that reminded Montgomery of his failure to secure the approaches to Antwerp, which was 'the real issue now at hand'. He then informed his unruly subordinate that the front was too long for one man to exercise close 'battle grip' on it, at the same time pointing out that 'it is quite often necessary to make concessions that recognize the existence of inescapable national differences'. He concluded by telling Montgomery that if he remained unhappy with the situation, he could refer the matter to higher authority. This was an invitation to a battle that the field marshal could not win, so great was the preponderance of American troops in the European theatre.

However, Montgomery refused to let the matter drop. On 30 November he demanded that one man only – that was, himself – should be given full operational control north of the Ardennes. Eisenhower, who was reluctant to wield the big stick, made an attempt to fudge the issue. He suggested that Monty would have priority in the north; however, there would be no halt to the advance in the south. This was a fair compromise, but it did not prevent Montgomery from appealing to Winston Churchill through the Chief of the Imperial General Staff (CIGS), Field Marshal Sir Alan Brooke.

At their invitation, Eisenhower met Churchill and Brooke in London on 12 December, when the Chief of Imperial General Staff strongly criticized what he described as the Supreme Commander's 'double front' strategy. He taxed Eisenhower with 'violating the principles of the concentration of force' and voiced his concern that he apparently did not propose to cross the Rhine until May 1945. Any further discussion was prevented by Churchill's ruminations on floating 'fluvial mines' down the Rhine. The next day, Churchill attempted to cheer the despondent Brooke, telling him that he had taken Eisenhower's side only because the Supreme Commander was a guest, a foreigner and in a minority of one.

Despite the hard pounding their armies had endured in the efforts to breach the West Wall, the Allied High Command still carried the infection of over-confidence from the sweeping victories of the late summer of 1944. As Christmas approached, Montgomery was anticipating a spot of leave. He told his troops: 'The enemy is fighting a defensive campaign on all fronts: his situation is that he cannot stage major offensive operations.'

In a playful mood, Montgomery demanded the prompt payment by Eisenhower of a £5 bet he had made with him that the war would not be over by Christmas. Eisenhower kept Monty waiting for the money for nine days, and by this time, there were far more important things preying on the Supreme Commander's mind.

Movement to the German assembly areas was accomplished principally by rail. The trains, concealed in tunnels or forests by day, moved at night to the appropriate area, unloaded and returned for another load before daylight. Air-raid warning stations were established near assembly areas, and when Allied aircraft were reported in the sector, the trains were rushed into tunnels. These air-raid precautions proved so effective that German losses to Allied air attacks totalled only 8 ammunition wagons in September, 11 wagons of ammunition and rations

Below: A Sonderkraftfahrzeug *(SdKfz) 250 series light armoured half track moves up to the Front. The vehicle was widely used in German armoured reconnaissance battalions. Its height of only 1.68m (5ft 6in) enabled it to take advantage of even limited cover.*

Above: M4 Shermans of US 9th Army find the going tough in November 1944. During the war no fewer than 49,234 Shermans were built, exceeding the combined tank output of the United Kingdom and Germany, and a tribute to American genius for mass production.

in October, and 4 wagons of fuel in November. In November, the assembly areas received a total of 3982 wagonloads of ammunition, fuel and rations, as well as horses, coal, weapons and equipment. Between September and December, the total loads delivered reached nearly 10,000 wagonloads and nearly 15,000 tonnes of supplies.

The logistical problems of moving the attack forces into position were huge. Divisions had to be transported to the assembly areas from as far away as Austria, East Prussia and Denmark. Bridges over the Rhine – which had recently been readied for demolition in order to prevent Allied crossings – now had to be strengthened again in order to carry the weight of the traffic which was heading West.

On 15 December, Hitler informed Model that the operation was now ready, and that 'he had received his last order' and that all commands were to be carried out unconditionally, to the last detail and to the lowest level. That same evening, Model confirmed that the Führer's orders had been passed on to Dietrich 'word for word'.

On the eve of his offensive Hitler could take great satisfaction from the fulfilment of the basic prerequisites he had specified when he had ordered the attack. The Western Front had withstood the Allied breakthrough attempts at Aachen and in Lorraine, although nine panzer and an equal number of infantry divisions had been sucked into battle and had suffered in varying degrees. Secrecy had been preserved, the weather was favourable and the Eastern Front had remained relatively quiescent, with the exception of the sector in Hungary. A colossal and universal effort had gone into the planning and the preparations for Germany's last offensive.

On paper the German order of battle for 'Autumn Mist' looked impressive. Between them, 6th and 5th Panzer Armies deployed eight panzer, one panzer-grenadier and two parachute divisions. Most of these units had fought in Normandy, enjoyed a battle-hardened leadership, and included in their forces non-commissioned officers (NCOs), junior officers and headquarters staff that had been brought up to strength following the Falaise debacle. These units included 1st, 2nd, 9th and 12th SS Panzer and 2nd, 9th, 116th and *Lehr* Panzer Divisions.

However, there had been much papering over the fissures that opened up in Germany's war-making capacity. One of the élite SS panzer formations, 2nd

Division *Das Reich*, was to be committed to battle at least 10 per cent below establishment. Its *Deutschland* Battalion was without motor transport, and its grenadiers were mounted on bicycles, most of these having to be repaired before they could be issued. There was also concern about the amounts of fuel available. The General Staff estimated that 12 fillings of petrol was the minimum amount needed to cover the duration of Operation 'Autumn Mist'. That number had been calculated on the estimation of one filling equalling 100km (62 miles) of driving on roads which were level and dry, not wet and bumpy from the excesses of the autumn weather. *Das Reich* received a total of only three issues of fuel for Operation 'Autumn Mist'. In addition, there was a shortage of winter clothing and boots for the troops of the division.

While every effort had been made to bring the SS panzer divisions up to strength, such first-line formations as 2nd and 116th Panzer deployed only 100 tanks each. *Panzer Lehr*, which had recently been in action against US 3rd Army, had suffered some heavy losses in tanks and men. On 15 December, this division could field only 57 MkIV and Panther tanks, although this was to some extent balanced by the addition of an assault gun brigade and two battalions of self-propelled tank destroyers.

The *Volksgrenadier* divisions that were to provide support for the armoured spearheads were short of

Below: A US rifleman armed with a Browning Automatic Rifle (BAR), a cross between a heavy rifle and a light machine gun popular among infantry, in the Ardennes. The American defences in the Ardennes were perilously weak and ill-prepared for the German onslaught to come.

Above: Hornisse *(Hornet) 88mm (3.46in) tank destroyers which were based on a MkIV panzer chassis. For the Ardennes, Hitler allotted to Army Group B the strategic armoured reserve of 2168 tanks and assault guns. Some 700 were allotted to 15th Army.*

Below: A German soldier with a Panzerfaust *antitank weapon. It consisted of a short steel tube containing a propelling charge with the tail stem of a shaped-charge bomb inserted into the tube's mouth. The tube was tucked beneath the arm and aim taken across the top of the bomb.*

Above: A German MG 42 machine gun which could be used as a squad or company support weapon. Designed for mass production, it had a rate of fire of 1200rpm and made a ripping sound when fired. Over 750,000 were made by 1945.

motor transport, poorly equipped, understrength and bolstered with 'ethnic' Germans who owed their nationality to frontier changes. For example, 5th Panzer Army's 66th *Volksgrenadier* Division, re-built almost from scratch from a division destroyed on the Eastern Front, contained many Czech and Polish conscripts who came from regions which had been annexed to the Reich, spoke no German at all and whose sympathies lay with the Allied armies they were about to engage. The 352nd *Volksgrenadier* Division, which had defended Omaha Beach and was now part of 7th Army, had been rebuilt on the ruins of its predecessor with *Luftwaffe* and navy replacements. This same army's 79th *Volksgrenadier* Division had been totally destroyed during the summer of 1944 on the Eastern Front, and its personnel now consisted principally of men who had been weeded out from rear-area headquarters.

In assembly areas close to the front line on the night of 15 December, commanders read out a message from Field Marshal von Rundstedt: 'Soldiers of the West Front! Your great hour has arrived. Large attacking armies have started against the Anglo-Americans. I do not have to tell you anything more than that. You feel it yourself. WE GAMBLE EVERYTHING! You carry with you the holy obligation to give everything to achieve things beyond human possibilities for our Fatherland and our Führer!'

In the SS panzer divisions, morale ran at a high. One SS trooper wrote back home to his sister with a glowing optimism: 'I write during one of the great hours before we attack … full of expectation for what the next day will bring. Everyone who has been here the last two days and nights (especially nights) who has witnessed hour after hour the assembly of our crack divisions, who has heard the constant rattling of Panzers, knows that something is up … we attack and will throw the enemy from our homeland. That is a holy task!'

Massacre at Malmédy

There's a big Kraut column coming, Colonel!
They've got tanks and half-tracks and armoured cars –
everything – and there's a helluva lot of them.
It looks like the whole German army!

US Military policeman near Malmédy, 17 December 1944

In the front-line positions in the Ardennes, American units could sense that something was afoot. For several nights, outposts of 106th Division had been reporting the noise of tracked vehicles. To the south, men of 28th Division noted that there were fresh and seemingly more disciplined troops opposite them. Further south down the American line, the G-2 of 4th Division, Lieutenant-Colonel Harry F. Hansen, had informed his commander Major-General Raymond O. Barton that there were large German formations in Bitburg. Barton had a suspicion that they might be preparing to launch a raid in force which was aimed at the American rear, perhaps in order to seize 12th Army's headquarters, located in Luxembourg City.

In the town of Diekirch, near the Our, worried civilians from front-line villages reported that German activity was on the increase. They were reassured by an American counter-intelligence unit; the Germans would not be coming back. Most of the civilians were not convinced. They moved on to the rear or sought beds with friends. At least one of the civilians on the move that night, Elise Dele, gave American intelligence officers a detailed picture of the build-up on the German side of the border.

Left: German troops barrel along an Ardennes road. The two men at the rear are paratroops. At this stage in the war one of the main logistical drawbacks in all large German formations was the multiplicity of vehicles they fielded, making for problems of repair and maintenance.

At 05:30 hours on 16 December, in the village of Hosingen, an American sentry from K Company, 110th Infantry, manning an observation post atop a concrete water tower on Skyline Drive, telephoned his company commander. He had something puzzling to report. Innumerable pinpoints of light had appeared in the German line. The sentry did not have long to wait for the explanation. Seconds later shells were crashing around him, and the observer realized that the pinpoints of light were the muzzle flashes of massed German artillery. It was the opening bombardment of the Battle of the Bulge: from mortars, multiple rocket launchers, 88mm (3.45in) howitzers and 355mm (14in) guns.

The bombardment cut telephone lines along the Front. When observers and platoon leaders reached for radios, they found the wavelengths jammed by the blare of German military bands. The shelling continued for an hour and then lifted to be replaced by the 'artificial moonlight' created by searchlights bouncing off the low cloud ceiling to illuminate American positions. The German infantry in white camouflage suits or mottled battle dress began to move forward in the spectral glow.

At the southern end of the Ardennes Front, on the seemingly quiet sector held by the men of 4th Infantry Division, there was no artificial moonlight and artillery fire fell only on positions held by the division's northernmost – 12th – regiment. Indeed, for battle-hardened veterans, the weight of the

German bombardment hardly compared with the heaviest fighting in Normandy. Nevertheless, it knocked out many of the telephone lines forward of battalion headquarters. The rest had been cut by German patrols. By late morning, German *Volksgrenadiers* had surrounded all five of the forward companies. F Company, some 60 men, were isolated in a resort hotel on the outskirts of Berdorf, 11km (7 miles) west of Echternach.

The Hotel Parc was sited on a high, windswept plateau near a spectacular rock formation known as 'Devil's Island'. Lieutenant John L. Leake and his men watched as a *Volksgrenadier* battalion marched into Berdorf. They were now cut off. They had taken a German prisoner but were only too well aware that in a few hours the roles might be reversed.

As darkness fell on 16 December, 12th Infantry continued to hold all its positions, with the exceptions of the outposts overrun in the first German

Below: A German soldier with a Panzerschreck *antitank rocket launcher (copied from the American bazooka) which fired an 8.8cm (3.45in) shaped-charge rocket to a range of 150m (500ft). It was also known as the 'stove pipe'* (Ofenrohr) *because of the smoke it emitted on firing.*

surge of the fog-shrouded early morning. Nevertheless, it was clear that the enemy was exerting ever-growing pressure. Major-General Raymond O. 'Tubby' Barton ordered that there was to be no retrograde movement in his sector. He decided to order the regiment at the extreme southern end of the line to release its reserve battalion to move north early on the morning of the 17th. He also directed most of his artillery to shift positions to support 12th Infantry and secured a promise from the commander of 9th Armored Division to despatch a company of medium tanks to arrive the next morning to augment his own depleted tank battalion. Finally he ordered an engineer battalion to be ready for commitment at only one hour's notice.

Immediately to the north of 4th Division, men of 9th Armored Division's 60th Armored Infantry Battalion held a 5km (3-mile) sector on a high plateau between the River Sure, in the north, and a stream in the south known as 'Black Ernz'. Here, the terrain of weathered sandstone rock resembled a Wild West location from an old Tom Mix silent movie. On the morning of the 16th, the armoured infantrymen found themselves facing an entire division, 276th *Volksgrenadier*. Following a 1000-round bombardment, the *Volksgrenadier* assault troops quickly infiltrated under cover of fog through the many deep ravines that cut the rugged terrain. Their objective was to gain high ground to the southwest some 13km (8 miles) from Luxembourg City.

Still farther north, on Skyline Drive, an elongated defensive front was held by 28th Infantry Division, which had been in action since the Normandy landings and had sustained such heavy casualties in the Hürtgen that its red, bucket-shaped keystone shoulder patch was dubbed the 'Bloody Bucket'. It was against 28th Division that von Manteuffel planned to launch 5th Panzer Army's main effort: two panzer corps, LVIII and XXXXVII, advancing in line abreast. Each of these corps fielded only two divisions, one *Panzergrenadier* and one *Volksgrenadier*, but Manteuffel held two panzer formations in reserve: the *Führer Begleit* brigade, an armoured unit built around Hitler's palace guard and never before tasked with front-line duty; and the *Panzer Lehr* Division, which Manteuffel intended to commit with XXXXVII Panzer Corps as soon as its *Volksgrenadier* Division had bridged the River Our. In this section of the front the ratio of attackers to defenders was approximately 10:1. Yet for the best part of a day, and unsupported by artillery fire, the outnumbered Americans grimly held on to their positions.

The weather also slowed German progress. Crossing the River Our, which was swollen by rain and melting snow, was an agonizingly slow process.

Urged on by Manteuffel, the German engineers completed the bridge for 2nd Panzer Division at 13:00 hours. The Division's MkIVs and Panthers inched down the hairpin bends on the eastern bank, which led to the bridge. Ten had crossed the Our when the next tank in the column misjudged the turn, crashed into the bridge and plunged into the river. It took nearly two hours to repair the damage, and it was late afternoon before the tanks could rumble across to the west bank. At about 16:00 hours, engineers of *Panzer Lehr* completed a bridge downstream at Germund. With two bridges across the Our, Manteuffel would soon be able to bring his armour to bear on the hard-pressed Americans as he raced on to his objectives, the towns of Clervaux and Bastogne. At about midnight, the American resistance in Marnach, astride the road to Clervaux, was

Above: A German soldier shoulders a Panzerfaust. *The gas expelled from the rear end of the tube countered the recoil. The weapon was effective against any wartime tank, provided the firer shot at the side or rear; against frontal armour, the* Panzerfaust *was marginal.*

silenced. The MkIVs of 2nd Panzer Division began to assemble in Marnach. At dawn they would strike down the road towards Clervaux and its two bridges spanning the River Clerve.

Moving up the line, on the sector north of 28th Division, on the Schnee Eifel, 106th Division underwent a baptism of fire. The division's centre and right had contained an attempt by 62nd *Volksgrenadier* Division to drive through to a bridge over the River Our at Steinebruck. The Americans had taken many casualties. The regiment on the left of the division's line, high in the north of the Schnee

THE BATTLE OF THE BULGE

Above: A Sturmgeschutz *assault gun of the* Panzer Lehr *Division fitted with Schürzen (side skirts) to counter shaped antitank charges. During the later stages of the war, German armoured vehicles received a coating of* Zimmerit *paste as a defence against magnetic charges.*

Eifel, had so far escaped attack. At the divisional headquarters in St Vith there was satisfaction at the way the green troops were holding up. However, little attention was paid to the danger on 106th's left flank, in the Losheim Gap.

In the Gap, a single cavalry reconnaissance formation, the battalion-sized 14th Cavalry Group, had sounded the alarm and delayed the enemy. But by 11:00 hours its commander, Colonel Mark A. Devine Jr, had decided to evacuate his headquarters at Manderfeld. Refugees were flooding into the town, and columns of German troops were threatening to cut it off. Devine got through on the telephone to divisional headquarters and obtained permission to withdraw from Manderfeld to bar a German advance on St Vith from the northeast, using Andler, and its vital road bridge, to anchor his line and deny the Germans access to the road down the valley of the Our behind the Schnee Eifel. That night Devine travelled to St Vith to talk with Major-General Allan W. Jones, commander of 106th Division, and try to get help. Devine was to stay in St Vith all night, waiting to speak to the divisional commander.

The remainder of the Ardennes front, from 106th Division's sector north to Monschau, was the

responsibility of 99th Infantry Division, which was another inexperienced formation that had been in the line for little more than a month. For some time they had been anticipating the arrival of a United Service Organizations (USO) troupe headed by Marlene Dietrich, who was scheduled to entertain the troops at divisional headquarters on the morning of the 16th. When Miss Dietrich and her troupe arrived, they were immediately hustled out of the danger zone. In the front line there was fierce hand-to-hand fighting. At the southern end of the division's front, mortarmen were setting their weapons at an almost vertical angle to drop shells on Germans who were hardly more than 11m (12yd) away.

The widespread disruption of the Americans' communications ensured that although fighting now raged along a 140km (85-mile) front, the units engaged believed that the fighting was local. It was not until the radio network was restored that communication was possible from division to battalion level. It was all but impossible for field commanders to form a clear picture of what was going on.

This paralysis extended to higher headquarters. After breakfast on 16 December, the commander of 12th Army Group, General Omar Bradley, had set off for a meeting with Eisenhower at SHAEF headquarters. As Bradley's olive drab Cadillac drove away though the murky streets of Luxembourg City, a routine briefing was taking place at his headquarters, at which it was noted that there had been no change at

Above: Marlene Dietrich, whose morale-boosting trip to the Ardennes sector was brought to an abrupt end by the start of 'Autumn Mist'. She was accompanied by the film actor David Niven, formerly an officer in the British Army in the 1930s, and now back in uniform.

the front. Nobody in Luxembourg City was aware of the nearby fighting; some of it was taking place barely 30km (20 miles) away.

At the headquarters of 1st Army, in the resort town of Spa, some 50km (30 miles) behind the Front, General Hodges admitted that the 'enemy line cannot be well defined as the front is fluid and somewhat obscure'. The situation was further confused by the fact that on 13 December one element of US V Corps, the experienced 2nd Infantry Division stationed at the northern end of the American line, had pushed into German territory through a narrow corridor in the front held by 99th Division. Its mission was to reach the Roer dams, but as reports of fighting on the front began to trickle into V Corps' headquarters, the corps commander, Major-General Leonard T. Gerow, became alarmed that 2nd Division ran the risk of being cut off. On the afternoon of the 16th, he called 1st Army headquarters to request permission for the withdrawal of 2nd Division. General Hodges, however, believed that the German attacks were localized and was unwilling to cede the ground gained during 2nd Division's penetration, and so he ordered Gerow to keep his men moving on and forwards.

The fighting along the American line on the morning of 16 December had quickly dissolved into a series of small-unit actions. One of these clashes was to exercise a crucial influence over the opening phase of 'Autumn Mist'. The village of Lanzerath was situated at the northern end of the Losheim Gap, overlooking a wide valley, the fortifications of the West Wall and the German village of Losheim. When the opening German bombardment lifted, part of Lanzerath's small garrison, including a squad of reconnaissance troops and the crews of two 76.2mm (3in) guns of the 820th Tank Destroyer Battalion, pulled out of the village. Left behind were the 18 men of one of 99th Division's Intelligence and Reconnaissance (IR) platoons. Led by First Lieutenant Lyle J. Bouck Jr, they occupied several log-covered foxholes in a copse of fir trees on the top of a hill a few hundred yards north of Lanzerath.

The bombardment had cut Bouck's telephone line, but he made radio contact with Major Robert L. Kriz at regimental headquarters and received orders to remain where he was and be on the alert for a German attack. Soon after the departure of the reconnaissance and tank destroyer troops, Bouck's men spotted a German column approaching along a road 90m (100yd) below their position. The Germans – men of 3rd Parachute Division – appeared remarkably relaxed, with their weapons slung over their shoulders, convinced that the bombardment had cleared Lanzerath of Americans.

Above: Lieutenant-General Courtney H. Hodges, commander of US 1st Army. As General Bradley's deputy in June 1944, Hodges organized the landings on Utah and Omaha Beaches. When Bradley was given command of 12th Army Group in August 1944, Hodges succeeded him.

Bouck decided to hold his fire until the main body of the column appeared, and waited until about 100 Germans had passed his positions. At this point a small girl ran into the Germans' path, shouted at them, and then ran off. Assuming that the little girl had betrayed their position, the Americans opened fire. The Germans took cover and a sharp firefight broke out in which the inexperience of the paratroops was to cost them dear. The fighting in Normandy had chewed up 3rd Parachute Division and the formation had been rebuilt in Holland, principally using rear-echelon *Luftwaffe* ground troops. Its officers were scarcely more experienced than the men they led into battle.

During a lull in the shooting, the Germans regrouped and attempted to drive Bouck's men off the hill. They had little or no fire support and no artillery, and had to charge at them uphill across an open, snowy field. They were brought to a sharp halt by a wire fence which was strung across an open field, directly in front of Bouck's position. Many were left hanging on the wire.

Meanwhile, Bouck was frantically appealing by radio to his regimental headquarters for artillery support. None was forthcoming. He was merely ordered to 'hold at all costs'. At about midday, the Germans removed their wounded under a white flag and then renewed their attack. As the afternoon wore on, Bouck's men began to run out of ammunition. As darkness fell, their positions were overrun in a flank attack and Bouck and his men taken prisoner. Bouck's runner, Private First Class William J. 'Sak' Tsakanikas, had suffered a terrible wound to his face, but was to survive the war. A German medical orderly attended to Tsakanikas' wound before the Americans were led into the dimly lit Café Scholzen. When the clock in the café struck midnight, Bouck reminded himself that today was his twenty-first birthday, unaware that on the hill outside Lanzerath he and his men had upset the German timetable upon which the success of 'Autumn Mist' depended.

Adolf Hitler had entrusted the major role in 'Autumn Mist' to 6th Panzer Army, commanded by Sepp Dietrich, whose deficiencies as an army commander were to be held in check by his chief of staff, Major-General Fritz Kraemer, a superb tactician Dietrich's army consisted of 12 divisions, but the hopes for success lay principally with just two of these divisions: 1st SS Panzer Division *Leibstandarte* and 12th SS Panzer *Hitler Jugend*. These élite formations enjoyed a reputation for extreme ruthlessness and had little or no time for the accepted rules of war. On the Eastern Front, where no quarter was given by either side, 1st SS Panzer had executed some 4000 Russian prisoners of war in a reprisal for the killing of 6 captured SS men by Russian military intelligence. In two separate incidents in Normandy in June 1944, 68 Canadian prisoners were shot out of hand after interrogation by 12th SS Panzer.

The SS Panzer divisions were to race through holes driven in the American lines by three of Dietrich's infantry divisions. Two roads running on parallel courses would then open the way to the Meuse and Antwerp. After clearing the Losheim Gap, 1st SS Panzer, commanded by Colonel Wilhelm Mohnke, was to take the southerly route from Lanzerath to the Meuse bridges at Huy, 80km (50 miles) away. To Mohnke's north, 12th SS Panzer, commanded by General Hugo Kraas, was to break through American positions on the Eisenborn Ridge, then drive west on a paved road. At the village of Malmédy, 12th SS Panzer was to swing northwest through the town of Spa to the Meuse bridges at Amay and Engis, near Liège.

The breakthrough in the north was of critical importance, as control of the Eisenborn Ridge and the Malmédy road would deny the Americans the

Above: A German infantry unit advances during the opening moves of 'Autumn Mist', which saw the first delays to the offensive's tight schedule. The soldiers are carrying a mix of weaponry, including a Panzerfaust, a Sturmgewehr *assault rifle, and a Kar 98K rifle.*

Below: A Tiger MkII Konigstiger *or 'King Tiger', which mounted a high-velocity 88mm (3.45in) L/71 gun. About 150 King Tigers fought in the Ardennes, employed in separate heavy tank battalions usually attached to a Panzer or an SS Panzer division.*

ability to rush reinforcements from the north to take the German advance in the flank. It was essential that the two panzer divisions maintained their momentum on a broad front to avoid their spearheads being separated from their supplies, isolated and rolled up by the Allies.

At the heart of 1st SS Panzer was a task force commanded by Lieutenant-Colonel Joachim Peiper. The son of a distinguished military family, the handsome, sophisticated 29-year-old Peiper was a glittering example of SS culture, a Nazi 'master of the universe'. Dietrich knew Peiper well, as the latter had served under him in Russia when Dietrich was in command of 1st SS Panzer Division *Leibstandarte*. In 1943, Dietrich was asked to come to the aid of 302nd Infantry Division, which was withdrawing under Soviet pressure with 1000 wounded. When the request was made, *Leibstandarte* was fighting to hold the line of the River Donets and was heavily engaged. Nevertheless, Dietrich withdrew a panzergrenadier battalion, commanded by Peiper, and

Below: A German MG 34 machine gun in action. Introduced to service in 1936, it was used with a bipod as a squad weapon and with a tripod in the sustained-fire role. Its exceptionally high quality made it difficult to manufacture. In 1943 it was superseded by the MG 42.

committed it to saving 302nd Infantry Division. Peiper crossed the Donets, beat off a succession of determined counterattacks by the Red Army and thrust on until he had linked arms with 302nd Infantry Division. Then both units withdrew to the Donets where the infantry safely crossed the river. Peiper, however, was left on the eastern bank because the ice was too thin to take the weight of his halftracks. He coolly swung his unit round, carved his way through the Red Army and reached a bridge capable of carrying his vehicles to safety. For this feat Peiper was awarded the Knight's Cross.

Peiper became a legend in the German Army, and the unit he commanded on the Eastern Front was dubbed the 'Blowtorch Battalion' because of his readiness to burn the villages of the enemy. Such early fame went to his head; Peiper was unafraid of contradicting the generals at conferences when he was the junior officer present.

For 'Autumn Mist', Peiper's ruthlessness in leading relatively small units that applied the maximum amount of force earned him the command of *Kampfgruppe* (Task Force) Peiper, reinforced to a strength of 5800 and with 72 MkIVs and Panthers and 30 MkVI King Tigers of 501st Heavy Panzer Battalion. The 68-tonne King Tigers were to travel at

the rear of Peiper's column until he reached open country near the Meuse. Peiper also had five flak tanks; a light flak battalion with self-propelled multiple 20mm (0.78in) guns; some 25 assault guns and self-propelled tank destroyers; an artillery battalion with towed 105mm (4.1in) howitzers; a battalion of SS panzergrenadiers; about 80 halftracks; a small detachment of reconnaissance troops; and two companies of engineers, although his planned speed of advance precluded the engineers carrying any bridge-building equipment. Also attached to Task Force Peiper was one of Skorzeny's four-man teams whose men were disguised as Americans, and another 'Greif' task force with its 12 Panthers unconvincingly disguised as US Sherman tanks.

Peiper got an indication of the role he had been chosen to play when on 10 December he was asked by Major-General Kraemer to determine whether a tank regiment could cover 80km (50 miles) in a night. Peiper borrowed a Panther and took it for a spin behind German lines. He already knew that a single tank on a clear road could cover the required distance, but he also knew that the same would not to be true of an entire regiment.

Peiper received his orders for 'Autumn Mist' from the commander of I SS Panzer Corps, General Hermann Priess, on 13 December. He was not best pleased with the route he was assigned, a secondary road that he complained bitterly was 'not for tanks but for bicycles'. His protests were stilled when he was informed that the Führer himself had selected the routes; they would be adhered to on pain of death, an example of the map generalship that had characterized Hitler's conduct of the war from 1942. There was another surprise in store for Peiper. The two trainloads of petrol allotted to 1st SS Panzer Division had not arrived in the assembly area. He would have to rely on captured American fuel. Two large Allied fuel dumps lay close to his line of advance, at Bullingen and to the south of Spa.

Priess also passed along an order of the day from Dietrich which repeated Hitler's exhortation to his senior commanders that 'Autumn Mist' was to be launched on a 'wave of terror and fright' in which human emotions must be put aside. Peiper later recalled that his soldiers were to be reminded of the thousands of German civilians who had died in Allied bombing raids, some of them being perhaps members of their own families. His subsequent recollection was that he was 'almost certain' that he was told prisoners of war should be shot 'where the local conditions of combat should so require it'. The provision was incorporated into the Task Force's orders for the attack. Although Peiper himself did not refer to it in his briefings to his subordinate commanders,

Above: The urbane and ruthless Joachim Peiper, whose Kampfgruppe *spearheaded 6th Panzer Army's breakthrough force. In 1946 Peiper was convicted and sentenced to death for war crimes, commuted to life imprisonment and then to 35 years. He was released in 1956.*

he did not need to spell this provision out. As he later would admit, 'they were all experienced officers to whom this was obvious'.

Thus, on the opening day of 'Autumn Mist', Peiper was ready to make one of the lightning thrusts through which he had gained his reputation. Instead, he found his path barred by a massive traffic jam on the narrow roads leading to the Losheim Gap, the result of a bridge near Losheim that had been demolished in September by the retreating Germans but which had been overlooked in the planning of 'Autumn Mist'. The infuriated Peiper ordered his tanks to 'push through rapidly and run down anything in the road ruthlessly', but he did not reach Losheim until 19:30 hours that night. At Losheim, Peiper received an order to divert westward through the village of Lanzerath, which would bring him near the scene of the stand made by

Above: A MkV Panther with spare tracks wrapped around its turret. The Panther was the German response to the Soviet T-34 and copied the former's sloped armour. After suffering serious teething problems in 1943, it acquired a formidable reputation; some 5500 were built.

Lieutenant Bouck and his men. Swinging west, Peiper drove through a German minefield, losing five of his precious tanks before he finally managed to get his column on the move.

Shortly before midnight, Joachim Peiper, now in a mounting fury, shouldered his way into the Café Scholzen in Lanzerath. A glance took in exhausted Germans asleep on the floor and Lieutenant Bouck and the grievously wounded Tsakinakas slumped under the café's cuckoo clock. Peiper demanded to know from his men what was going on. This picturesque tableau of exhaustion was not his way of waging war. Buttonholing the commander of 9th Parachute Regiment, Colonel Helmüt von Hofmann, Peiper could hardly believe his ears when he was told that the colonel was delaying his attack until the morning, the reason being that the woods between Lanzerath and Honsfeld were heavily fortified, defended in battalion strength and mined.

Peiper ploughed on. Had Hofmann personally reconnoitred the American positions? While the hapless Hofmann hummed and hawed, Peiper insisted that the colonel reinforce him with one of his parachute infantry battalions. Peiper was determined to press on with his thrust through the lines.

It was nearly 04:00 hours when the lead elements of *Kampfgruppe* Peiper – two Panthers and three halftracks – moved off in the direction of Honsfeld. Following them were four MkIV Flak tanks, each equipped with a 37mm (1.46in) cannon, and two Flak wagons mounting quadruple 20mm (0.78in) armament. Then came more halftracks carrying Panzergrenadiers and tanks with paratroops clinging to the decks. Flank protection as the column moved through the forest between Lanzerath and Honsfeld was provided by a company of paratroops.

A flicker of resistance came from two platoons of US 394th Infantry Regiment occupying a farm near the road and the surrounding forest, but they were quickly silenced by the quad-20s on the Flak halftracks. Peiper's column met no more Americans until it reached a junction near Honsfeld, where his lead tank locked on to a stream of US vehicles – trucks, ammunition carriers, prime movers towing artillery pieces – heading into Honsfeld.

At about 05:00 hours the lead German tank crept slowly into the outskirts of Honsfeld, past an armoured car posted to raise the alarm if the Germans arrived outside the town. As the tank rumbled by, Sergeant John Creel, the commander of the armoured car crew, made out a swastika on its side. Creel tried to open fire but he was prevented from doing so by the trailer attached to his armoured car. A short burst of firing followed as the German tank encountered yet more Americans. Then confusion broke out as Creel and his crew struck back into Honsfeld in order to raise the alarm.

The two lead Panthers of *Kampfgruppe* Peiper nosed their way cautiously into the heart of Honsfeld, followed by three halftracks with Peiper riding in one of them. Soon they were surrounded by parked American vehicles. The machine-gunners in the tanks and on the halftracks opened fire, hosing vehicles and buildings with bullets as they moved through the centre of Honsfeld. Behind them

more halftracks were moving into the town, disgorging their Panzergrenadiers as they went.

Some of the Americans managed to flee in their jeeps and halftracks, dodging German fire as they went. Others, wakened from sleep by the eruption of *Kampfgruppe* Peiper in the middle of Honsfeld, decided to surrender. It was then that the killing began. In one house near the centre of the town, an SS officer forced eight Americans, blinking with sleep, out of their billet, lined them up against a wall and then mowed them down with an automatic weapon. From another house, five American soldiers emerged under a white flag. Four were immediately cut down and the fifth, who was wounded, was despatched under a tank's tracks. In another part of Honsfeld, 18 men of 612th Tank Destroyer Battalion emerged, after a brief firefight, with a tablecloth as a

Below: Panzergrandiers of 2nd SS Panzer Division Das Reich *race across a road during the opening phase of Operation 'Autumn Mist'.* Das Reich *had a reputation for brutality gained from the fighting on the Eastern Front and in France in 1944.*

Above: MkV Panthers of 6th Panzer Army grind along a snowbound road in the Ardennes. The Panther had a road speed of 55km/h (34mph). With 120mm (4.7in) armour, it mounted a 75mm (2.95in) L/70 gun and two 7.92mm (0.31in) machine guns.

Below: The shock of the German attack clearly shows on these men of a Quartermaster's Company who were caught in the path of the German advance. These men were lucky, as they managed to evade the enemy; others would spend the last months of the war in a prison camp.

Above: American troops surrendering to men of 1st SS Panzer Division Leibstandarte *Adolf Hitler during the latter's advance. Until the offensive's momentum was lost, the initial phase of 'Autumn Mist' saw a number of American prisoners taken by the Germans.*

flag of surrender. Two of them were shot as they stood with their hands raised, and a third man, Staff Sergeant Billy F. Wilson, managed to run off and hide in the fields. He was to survive.

Another group of some 100 men, most of them from 612th Battalion, were fired upon as they stood in a tightly packed group with their arms raised. A witness, Private First Class William T. Hawkins, claimed that up to 30 of these men were killed. Then, as abruptly as it had started, the firing died away and the survivors were marched down the road towards Lanzerath. However, their torment was only beginning. Tanks and halftracks attempted to run them down. They were struck by rifle butts wielded by soldiers riding on the tanks. When an American fell, the guards made no move to help him. Two more prisoners were machine-gunned at random. There was no relief, though one gallant teenage German soldier intervened to prevent an officer taking a potshot at a group of prisoners. The young soldier barred his way with outstretched hands, and the officer moved off.

Peiper then decided to change the direction of his march, making a detour to Bullingen, which lay on 12th SS Panzer's route. Peiper had been told that there was an American fuel dump here. Having

released the paratroops he had commandeered at Lanzerath, he started for Bullingen, which served as a centre for troops supporting 99th and 2nd Divisions. Just outside the town there was an improvised airfield for the observation pilots of 2nd and 99th Divisions and their small L-5 spotter aircraft. Here, with the aid of reluctant American groundcrew, the Germans were able to help themselves to some 230,000 litres (50,000 gallons) of fuel. In the town's big open square, used as a cattle market in more peaceful times, Peiper's tanks and halftracks found the fuel they so desperately needed in a depot only recently established by 2nd Division's Quartermaster Company. Again, captured Americans were forced to refuel the German vehicles. *Kampfgruppe* Peiper had taken another 200 prisoners in the brief fight for Bullingen, but only one, Private Bernard Pappel, had been shot in cold blood.

To clear the road to Bullingen for 12th SS Panzer Division, Peiper pulled his troops out of the town and resumed his southward progress. By noon, the

Above: A German convoy crosses a bridge thrown up by engineers while a light antiaircraft gun stands ready to counter Allied air attack. The unforgiving schedule for 'Autumn Mist' was predicated on maximum bad weather ensuring minimum air activity by the Allies.

head of his column was approaching the crossroads hamlet of Baugnez, 4km (2.5 miles) south of Malmédy and an important road junction. The roads were now jammed with American vehicles travelling in all directions. From the east came a stream of trucks, jeeps and staff cars plunging away from the buckling front line. Swimming hard against the current were combat units going to the battlefront.

One of these was Battery B of 285th Field Artillery Observation Battalion, a unit that was threading its way from the Hürtgen Forest in the north to the town of Vielsalm, 8km (5 miles) to the south of Peiper's march. They were on collision course with *Kampfgruppe* Peiper, which trapped them in Baugnez just after 13:00 hours. A firefight erupted which was halted by the arrival of Peiper, who roared into Baugnez in an American jeep, furious

that Battery B's trucks – potentially so useful to his Task Force – had been shot to pieces. The Americans were rounded up from the ditch in which they had taken cover. The men who had attempted to escape over the fields had been picked off.

Peiper's men then herded their disarmed prisoners together in small groups, taking care to relieve them of many of their valuables: rings, watches, gloves and cigarettes. Peiper had regained control over his men, and his tanks and halftracks began moving in the direction of Ligneuville. Peiper left in a halftrack with the commander of his Panzergrenadier battalion, Major Josef Diefenthal.

The prisoners, some 130 of them including men from other units, were herded into a field next to the main highway, the N-23. There they stood in about eight rows, covered by two MkIV tanks, their hands above their heads. Few were eager to remain in the front row and there was some jostling. There was, however, little panic; the Americans believed that they were awaiting transport to the rear. They would spend Christmas as prisoners of war.

Then the firing began. The men were so tightly packed together that they went down in an accordion-like wave. One of the Germans shouted 'Kill them all!' and the machine guns on both tanks opened up. The men who survived the initial burst of fire hurled themselves to the ground, burying their faces in the mud and trying to squirm under the mound of corpses around them.

As the bullets raked the piles of prostrate bodies, a terrible noise went up, screams, groans and sighs blending together in a nightmarish lowing. The firing lasted about 15 minutes before most of the Germans moved off. But bullets continued to slam into the mass of bodies, fired by passing Germans. Meanwhile men of an SS Pioneer Company moved through the field to finish off survivors. Any sign of life was confirmed by a swift kick in the groin. Some Germans cruelly persuaded men to speak up by offering them medical treatment. One even allowed an aid man to administer medical treatment to a fellow prisoner, and then shot them both.

Some men survived the carnage. One of them was Sergeant Kenneth F. Ahrens, who had been

shot in the back and his uniform was so soaked in blood from his and others' wounds that he escaped examination by the Pioneers. He recalled:

'I could hear them walking down amongst the boys that were lying there. Naturally there was a lot of moaning and groaning, and some of the boys weren't dead yet. You would hear a stray shot here and a stray shot there; they were walking around, making sure there was nobody left. Each time they would hear somebody moan, they would shoot him; and there was one particular time when I could feel a footstep right alongside of me, where one of the boys laid across the back of me, or this side of me, and they shot him. But why they didn't shoot me I don't know ... Every once in a while a tank or a half-track would roll by and turn their guns on us, just for a good time. I mean they were laughing, they were having a good time.'

Below: American troops are marched into captivity during the Battle of the Bulge. US troops taken at Malmédy anticipated a similar fate: Christmas as prisoners of war. However, the men of Kampfgruppe Peiper *had a different outcome in mind on 17 December 1944.*

Left: Bodies of the fallen at Malmédy. Immediately after their execution by men of Kampfgruppe *Peiper, they had been covered by snow. News of the massacre was given wide publicity and helped to stiffen American resolve against the Germans.*

Ahrens was one of the few who survived. After waiting for what seemed like several lifetimes, he heard an American voice whispering 'Let's go!' Ahrens staggered to his feet and, with bullets whistling over his head, made the safety of the treeline on the edge of the field. Others who made a run for it headed for a café, which was set on fire by the Germans. Those who fled the flames were machine-gunned as they emerged. Some of the survivors staggered into the outposts of 291st Engineers Combat Battalion, whose commander, Colonel David E. Pergrin, sent a sobering report up the line: 86 soldiers had been killed in cold blood while being held as prisoners of war. Pergrin might have added that a number of Belgian civilians had also died in *Kampfgruppe* Peiper's rampage. One of the most poignant deaths was that of 16-year-old Erna Collas,

ordered to guide five SS troopers from Honsfeld to Bullingen. Erna's body was found in the spring of 1945 in a shallow grave on the road to Bullingen.

The mayhem which had been caused by *Kampfgruppe* Peiper was not repeated by Skorzeny's 'Greif' commandos. Only one of his three large task forces was launched on its original mission of seizing the Meuse bridges. Skorzeny's men rode well to the rear of Peiper's long 26km (16-mile) column and, to that combative commander's dismay, seemed unwilling to fulfil its mission and make a lightning dash for the bridge at Huy. Since he had no operational control over them, Peiper could only fume at the 'Greif' commandos' insouciance. The other two 'Greif' task forces which had been attached to 12th SS Panzer Division were simultaneously making an equally tortuous progress to their objective.

Below: American military policemen check the credentials of vehicles passing through a crossroads in the Ardennes. The 'Greif' commandos had an effect far greater than their numbers, causing panic behind the Allied lines and forcing Eisenhower to have a significant bodyguard.

Above: The end of the line for one of Skorzeny's 'Greif' commandos, executed following their capture on 18 December. Before their execution, the 'Greif' commandos were granted a final request: to hear German nurses in a nearby cell singing Christmas carols.

Nevertheless, on 16 and 17 December Skorzeny despatched a total of 10 four-man teams, masquerading as Americans with German uniforms under their battledress, to penetrate the enemy lines. The 'Greif' commandos achieved only limited success in their mission. One group reached a road junction on the Hautes-Fagnes known as Mont Rigi. They set about changing road signs and succeeded in sending a battalion of 1st Infantry Division on a roundabout route to Waimes by way of Malmédy. The 'Greif' commandos also cut many telephone lines, but this caused little disruption compared to the wire-cutting work of German patrols carried out before 'Autumn Mist' opened, or the efforts of German-speaking civilians hostile to the Allies.

The first of Skorzeny's teams to fall into American hands was a unit attached to *Kampfgruppe* Peiper. Within an hour of setting off they were stopped and questioned by a military policeman (MP). Discrepancies in their equipment and clothing aroused the MP's suspicions: one of the commandos

wore a regulation belt, but none of the others had one; none wore leggings or combat boots; nor did they carry the customary invasion currency but had only dollars and pounds in their pockets. Their fate was sealed when they revealed that they all carried the German soldier's personal document, the *Soldbuch.* When the 'Greif' commandos had been formed, Skorzeny sought legal advice on their status were they to be captured, and was assured that their mission was a legitimate *ruse de guerre* provided that they did not fight in their US uniforms. He had been misinformed. All captured 'Greif' commandos were to be shot by the Americans.

A second team was captured on 18 December by an American unit manning a roadblock on the route running into Malmédy from the Baugnez junction. The team had captured two Americans and were bringing them into what they mistakenly thought was German-held Malmédy. But their prisoners raised the alarm and the 'Greif' commandos' mission ended in a hail of bullets, leaving one of them dead.

Two teams claiming to have penetrated the Meuse returned to the German lines barely 24 hours later, having accomplished little more than some surreptitious sightseeing. Another team reached the Meuse at a bridge equidistant between Huy and Namur,

where they were detained by another suspicious MP. Their leader, Lieutenant Gunther Schulz, sang like a canary. He informed his captors that General Eisenhower was one of Skorzeny's principal targets, and the commandos' aim had been to penetrate SHAEF headquarters in order to carry out the assassination of the Supreme Commander.

Skorzeny's name alone was sufficient to convince American counter-intelligence men that there was some substance to Schulz's story. A sceptical Eisenhower was put into the picture on 18 December and reluctantly agreed to stepped-up security measures, including the deployment of a double, Lieutenant-Colonel Baldwin B. Smith.

Above: A German paratrooper moves forward. Serving with 6th Panzer Army was 3rd Parachute Division, which had been nearly destroyed in Normandy and rebuilt in Holland, mainly from rear-echelon Luftwaffe troops. The men and the officers were inexperienced.

General Bradley was also forced to submit to a tight security regime. His personal aircraft was moved from a civilian airstrip to a secure military base and he was ordered not to travel by limousine. He was now to ride in a jeep without a general's stars on the bumper and with a heavy escort. The stars were also removed from his helmet, a precaution unlikely to bother the self-effacing Bradley, whose battledress was strictly standard issue.

The fear that the rear areas were swarming with Skorzeny's desperados led to a heightened emphasis on security. It was not enough to know the day's password at a roadcheck. Many a senior officer, including General Bradley, struggled with grillings on American baseball heroes, Hollywood stars' wives and husbands and obscure state capitals.

By Christmas Eve, the threat posed by the commandos had dissipated. On that day four men in a jeep burst through a British roadblock near Dinant only to hit a necklace of mines pulled across the road when the jeep failed to stop. There was immediate consternation when the troops manning the roadblock saw that the dead occupants of the jeep were apparently Americans. There were sighs of relief when closer examination revealed the German uniforms underneath the American overcoats.

The 'Greif' commandos had failed. The paratroops led by Colonel von der Heydte were no more successful. Frustrated that he had been given only five days in which to prepare the operation, von der Heydte asked Model to cancel it. Model's response was to ask whether, in von der Heydte's opinion, the mission stood a 10 per cent chance of success. The colonel agreed that it did. In that case, observed Model, the mission must be attempted, since the chances for success for Operation 'Autumn Mist' itself stood at no more than one in ten.

This was small comfort to von der Heydte, who was concerned about the inexperience of the men under his command. Although the *Luftwaffe* crews who were to fly to the drop zone were members of the celebrated 'Stalingrad Squadron', which in 1942 had flown supplies to the besieged 6th Army, the only member of the unit who had actually been over Stalingrad during that terrible battle was its commanding officer. The pilots under his command had no experience of airborne operations; indeed, they had no actual experience of combat and furthermore had never even flown their planes at night. Von der Heydte's heart sank when he heard this.

He was, however, in an exposed position. It would have been unwise of him to balk at the task in hand, as he was a cousin of Colonel Count Claus von Stauffenberg, and a cloud of suspicion hung over him. As a result, when the airborne operation was aborted on the night of 15 December – most of the paratroops had failed to arrive at their designated airfields because their trucks had no fuel – an officer from 6th Army headquarters had been

despatched in order to establish if von der Heydte himself might have sabotaged the operation. General Kraemer's order to jump on the 16th forestalled this investigation, but also ended von der Heydte's fervent hope that the mission might be called off.

In the small hours of 17 December, 112 Ju 52s took off from two airfields near Paderborn. Von der Heydte was in the lead aircraft and would jump first. To add to his long list of woes, his right arm was in a splint, having been injured in an accident several weeks before. The transports ran into heavy antiaircraft fire as they approached the drop zones; in order to maintain formation, they had been forced to fly with their landing lights on.

Over the drop zone, von der Heydte – his injured arm strapped to his side – leapt boldly into the night. He was knocked unconscious when he came to earth, and when he finally came to his senses he found himself alone. He struggled to the designated rendezvous – an important road junction – to find just 20 of his 1200 men. The force had been widely scattered; one group of 200 men had come down miles behind the German lines near Bonn; others had landed near Aachen in the sector held by US 9th Army. The most successful airdrop that night involved 300 decoy dummies which were dressed as paratroopers and released near Eisenborn Ridge. This was mistaken for a genuine airborne operation by the Americans, and this mistake would tie up a substantial number of Allied troops who searched in vain for non-existent Germans.

Three hours after executing their jump, von der Heydte's force had risen to 150 men, but it was clear that this depleted group would not be able to hold the road junction against any kind of American counterattack. Von der Heydte decided to lie low near the junction and bide his time until the arrival of German armour. The airborne troops waited for five days, spending their precious time watching units of three American divisions as they rolled past unhindered on the same highway that von der Heyte and his men had been ordered to cut.

Abandoning the fruitless vigil, von der Heydte ordered his men to split into groups of three and make their way back to the German lines. He set out with his executive officer and a runner, sleeping in forests by day and marching by night towards Monschau, located at the northern end of the Ardennes Front. This was the objective that 6th Army had been tasked with capturing on the first day of Opearation 'Autumn Mist', but it was still in American hands. Seven days after setting out from Paderborn, von der Heydte and his men were to become American prisoners. Germany's last airborne operation of the war had ended in total failure.

CHAPTER FIVE

The Battle for Eisenborn Ridge

That's no spoiling attack!

General Eisenhower, 16 December 1944

In the northern sector of the Ardennes, the most critical battle developed around the boomerang-shaped Eisenborn Ridge, near the German border, where German Ju 52s had successfully dropped 300 dummies, the only successful element in von der Heydte's doomed operation. And just as von der Heydte had found, success or failure at this point was determined by the struggle for road junctions.

Eisenborn Ridge dominated two roads leading into Bullingen, feeding the northern route to the Meuse which ran through Malmédy. *Kampfgruppe* (Task Force) Peiper had made a detour into this area and then had pulled out after its successful fuel foraging. It was now imperative that Dietrich's 6th Army seize control of the feeder roads in order to launch 12th SS Panzer Division westwards.

The most important feeder route in this sector ran through the border village of Losheimergraben and then veered northwest to Bullingen. To clear this road for his armour, Dietrich tasked 12th *Volksgrenadier* Division, the most experienced infantry formation in 6th Army, with the taking of Losheimergraben. A second feeder road ran through the adjacent villages of Krinkelt and Rocherath and then swung southwest to Bullingen. To prevent

Left: MkV Panthers of 12th SS Panzer Division rumble forward. In a one-on-one clash with a Sherman, the Panther had the upper hand. Although the Sherman fought on equal terms with a German MkIV, it could knock out a Panther only with a shot to the latter's side or rear.

American artillery from interdicting the main road to Malmédy, Dietrich had ordered 277th *Volksgrenadier* Division, a weak formation containing many ethnic Germans, to seize Krinkelt and Rocherath and over-run the Ridge. Dietrich intended to hold 12th SS Panzer behind the front until both of these roads had been opened up by his infantry.

Dietrich was confident that these moves would unleash 12th SS Panzer Division. The American division opposite him, 99th Infantry, was inexperienced and extended over a long front which could have accommodated three more divisions. However, Dietrich's confidence had been fuelled by a critical error of German intelligence. He had been told that the battle-hardened US 2nd Division was resting in a rear area. In fact, most of 2nd Division was attacking into Germany only a few miles north of Dietrich's planned thrusts around the Eisenborn Ridge.

On the morning of 16 December, after the German bombardment lifted, Dietrich ordered his infantry forward. At Losheimergraben a company of 3rd Battalion, 394th Infantry Regiment, 99th Division, was stationed around the town's small railway station. The men had not been unnerved by the German bombardment. Indeed they were more concerned with the arrival of a field kitchen and were anticipating their first hot meal in several days.

The chow line had not yet formed when somebody noticed a group of about 50 men emerging from the fog on the other side of the railway track.

At first it was assumed that they were men of the company's weapons platoon arriving for breakfast, but when orders shouted in German floated over the air, the Americans dropped their mess kits, reached for their rifles and opened fire on the soldiers. They were, in fact, the advance guard of the leading battalions of 12th *Volksgrenadier*'s 27th Regiment.

The battle for Losheimergraben raged all day. When darkness fell in the late afternoon, the Americans still held the railway station, having stood firm against the *Volksgrenadiers* and the tanks that Dietrich had ordered in during the afternoon. By

Below: A map showing the German thrusts in the northern sector over the first three days of 'Autumn Mist', with the failed parachute landings and Eisenborn Ridge clearly marked. The dogged defence of Rocherath and Krinkelt caused a significant delay to the German timetable.

nightfall, Dietrich had committed all of 12th SS Panzer Division's tanks not only to the fight for Losheimergraben but also to the struggle for Krinkelt–Rocherath 10km (6 miles) to the north. At midnight Major-General Walter E. Lauer, commander of 99th Division, reported to V Corps headquarters that 99th Division was holding not far from its original line and that the situation was in hand. Lauer seemed confident, although he knew of the order issued by von Rundstedt – 'we gamble everything!' – as it had been captured and handed in by a soldier of 394th Infantry's A Company. Lauer could hardly have believed that his division was confronted with a local reaction to the attack on the Roer dams.

The commander of V Corps, Major-General Leonard T. Gerow, remained anxious. Gerow had not yet obtained permission from General Hodges to

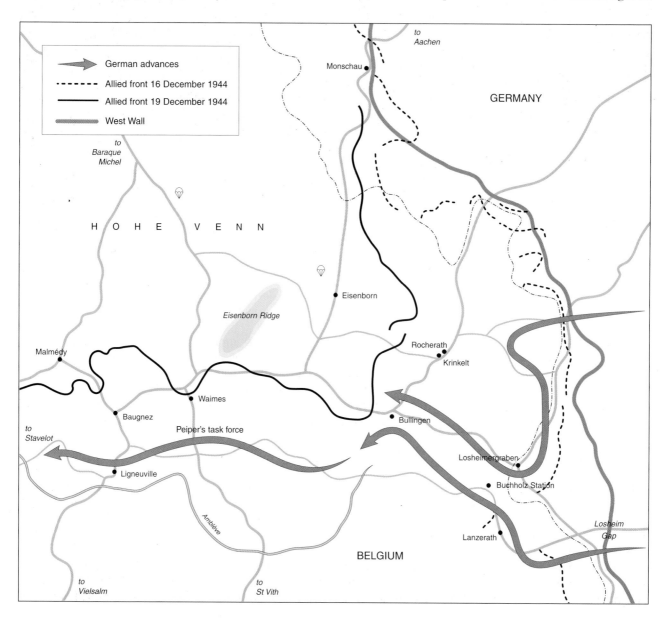

withdraw 2nd Division from its exposed position and he was fearful that if the division was forced to retreat to the Eisenborn area, its route along the Krinkelt–Rocherath road would be cut by the Germans. It was imperative to hold the two villages until the scattered units of 2nd and 99th Divisions could be brought back to strong defensive positions along Eisenborn Ridge. Reluctant to exceed his authority, Gerow did what he could. The reserve regiment of 2nd Division – 23rd – was brought forwards from the town of Eisenborn. One battalion was rushed to Hunningen, a short distance from the Losheimergraben crossroads, and the other to the forest east of Krinkelt–Rocherath.

It was not until the morning of the 17th that General Hodges realized that Gerow's front was in grave danger and that 2nd Division was under threat. He also grasped that Peiper's eruption on the southern flank of 99th Division's front threatened to cut off both 99th and 2nd Divisions from the rear. He therefore instructed Gerow to defend his corps as he saw fit. He also sent an urgent message requesting

Above: Panzergrenadiers examine a haul of American vehicles of 30th Division on the northern shoulder of the Bulge in the Malmédy/Stavelot sector. The 30th Division fought in Normandy in 1944 and distinguished itself during the German counterattack at Mortain and at Aachen.

help from 1st Infantry Division, which was at that point taking a welcome rest near Aachen.

At 19:30 hours on 17 December, Gerow ordered the commander of 2nd Division, Major-General Walter M. Robertson, to withdraw. This came as no surprise to Robertson, who had already prepared a detailed plan for a withdrawal in daylight and under enemy fire. Dubbed 'skinning the cat', this was a movement fraught with peril in which the attacking 2nd Division troops would fall back through their rear units which would then cover their withdrawal. The rear units, now in front, would then fall back in turn, covered by the attacking units until the entire force had gained the relative safety of Krinkelt–Rocherath. While 2nd Division held off 6th Panzer Army, all the men of 99th Division would withdraw through 2nd Division to establish a line of defence on Eisenborn Ridge. There they were to be joined by 2nd Division.

In the rugged Ardennes terrain, in the depths of winter, the possibilities for murderous confusion were all too evident. If the formations were in close contact with the Germans, covering fire from the rear units would be impossible. If units became inextricably muddled in the withdrawal, the chain of command would then break down.

Robertson took personal command of the withdrawal, even directing traffic as 9th Regiment leapfrogged back through 38th Regiment along the road to Rocherath. Meanwhile, in the early hours of the 17th, German tanks and infantry launched new attacks on the two 99th Division regiments and 2nd Division's reserve regiment. A renewed attack by 12th *Volksgrenadier* shovelled one of 99th's battalions from Losheimergraben and forced another to withdraw, leaving its wounded behind.

At about the same time, a reconnaissance tank company from *Kampfgruppe* Peiper's spearhead was

Below: The crew of a M7 105mm (4.1in) howitzer motor carriage from Gerow's V Corps stands guard against the enemy at the roadside as an M4 Sherman moves along the road. The M7 self-propelled howitzer was based on the chassis of the M4 Sherman.

threatening 2nd Division's headquarters at the village of Wirtzfeld. If Peiper drove on to Wirtzfeld and Krinkelt–Rocherath, he would roll up 2nd and 99th Infantry Divisions from the flank. If he thrust on to Bütgenbach and swung north along the road to Eisenborn, he would take the two divisions and their attachments – as many as 30,000 men – in the rear.

This was precisely what Major-General Lauer feared. Lauer later wrote: 'The enemy had the key to success within his hands but he did not know it.' Major-General Robertson was of the same mind. Just before 07:00 hours on 17 December, Robertson telephoned the commander of 2nd Division's forward headquarters, Lieutenant-Colonel Matt C. Konop, from a house on the edge of Wirtzfeld. Robertson told Konop that German tanks had broken through and were making for Bullingen. He wanted Konop to lay his hands on every man and gun he could to form 'a last ditch defence of the CP'. Konop formed an improvised defence line on the southern fringe of Wirtzfeld composed of cooks, clerks, drivers and military policemen. The line was stiffened by the presence of divisional artillery commander Brigadier-General John H. Hinds, who positioned a battery of 105mm (4.1in) and another of 155mm (6.1in) howitzers to fire on the approaches to Wirtzfeld from Bullingen. In addition, there were some 57mm (2.25in) antitank guns, and four half-tracks with quad .50 (12.7mm) machine guns.

At about 08:00 hours, five German tanks and half-tracks loomed out of the mist on the Bullingen road, crossing a ridge 915m (1000yd) outside Wirtzfeld. Simultaneously, Konop's defence force received the reinforcement of five self-propelled tank destroyers of the attached 644th Tank Destroyer Battalion. In short order the destroyers knocked out four of the German tanks and a halftrack, and the others turned tail and withdrew to Bullingen.

The situation, however, was critical near Krinkelt–Rocherath where 12th *Volksgrenadier*, reinforced by tanks of 12th SS Panzer, were battering 99th Division. The Americans yielded ground grudgingly, even when the Germans brought up five Tigers. Stubborn resistance by men of 23rd Regiment enabled 9th and 38th Regiments to withdraw in good order to Krinkelt–Rocherath, where they were joined by the survivors of 23rd Regiment. As darkness closed in, German armour was slashing at the American lines. The German tanks broke through several times, only to be forced back by determined counterattacks. Through Rocherath poured a constant flow of 99th Division troops, making their way to Eisenborn Ridge. The units became so entangled with each other that one 2nd Division commander counted men from at least 16 different units fighting

Above: Although the Germans fought desperately hard, they would eventually be unable to take Eisenborn Ridge from its American defenders. The American troops lacked proper winter combat gear, and improvised clothing was commonplace.

under him. Throughout the night the Americans clung to the twin villages.

At about 07:00 hours on the morning of the 18th, the fighting erupted again with fresh savagery. On the outskirts of Rocherath, a 2nd Division company commander, First Lieutenant Stephen E. Trupper, radioed in that tanks and infantry had overrun his position and called for artillery fire on his own fox-holes. A full battalion of guns responded to his request with a bombardment that lasted for 30 minutes. Many Germans, caught in the open, were killed. When the bombardment lifted, there was no further word from Trupper, although 12 members of his company eventually straggled in with the survivors of 1st Battalion, 9th Regiment, commanded by Lieutenant-Colonel William D. McKinley. Colonel McKinley had gone into the fight for Rocherath with approximately 600 men. He fell back with 217. Not only had they enabled two battalions of 38th Infantry Regiment to gain the safety of Rocherath

Below: Victorious American troops examine a MkV Panther that they have managed to disable. A bazooka would only be effective against a Panther if fired at its rear or side, as the tank's frontal armour was too thick for the bazooka rocket to penetrate.

and to mount a defence, they also left the ground around the village littered with German dead and the burnt-out hulls of 17 tanks and tank destroyers.

Krinkelt–Rocherath had become a killing ground for German armour. Armoured commanders were loathe to risk their vehicles in street fighting, where they were exceptionally vulnerable to prowling bazooka teams, concealed tanks and tank destroyers, the concentrated fire of American artillery and mines. The last two threats rarely destroyed a tank but could disable it, leaving it to be finished off by bazooka teams. The 75mm (2.95in) guns on the Shermans and the 76mm (3in) cannon on the towed and self-propelled tank destroyers were seldom effective against the frontal armour of Panthers, but handled by experienced crews they could disable the enemy with a well-placed shot to the side or

rear. In Rocherath, two Shermans accounted for five Tigers as they lumbered past, immobilized in a lane, and exposing their vulnerable rear armour.

Concealed in the upper storeys of houses, American infantry were well-placed to fire into an open turret or rear deck, blocking the street to any further tank movement. The crews of disabled tanks rarely escaped the attention of the bazooka teams who would pick them off as they emerged to make their escape from the turret or escape-hatch.

In the confusion of the fighting, the entanglement between 2nd and 99th Divisions had become so comprehensive that 99th temporarily ceased to exist as an integral force. General Gerow ordered Major-General Robertson to take over as the temporary commander of both divisions. By the late afternoon of 18 December the last organized units of 99th Division had withdrawn through 2nd Division's lines, completing the 'skinning of the cat'. In three days of intense fighting, they had held off three divisions of 6th Panzer Army and prevented German armour from breaking through to the Malmédy road.

Below: American infantry examine a knocked-out King Tiger, which appears to have surrendered to them, judging by the white flag on the turret. The most likely reason is that the tank had become immobilized without infantry support, leaving it vulnerable to the American GIs.

Above: An American artillery barrage under way in the Ardennes. Artillery was feared by both sides, and was responsible for the majority of casualties during World War II. In the absence of air cover, the Americans' artillery was an important factor in the battle.

Below: A German halftrack moves past a knocked-out American M10 tank destroyer. A number of Panther tanks were unconvincingly converted to look like M10s by the Germans for the purposes of their deception campaign at the start of 'Autumn Mist'.

Sepp Dietrich was forced to abandon his attempt to seize the twin villages. On the night of 18 December he ordered 12th SS Panzer to seize the road to Malmédy from the south. This change of tactic came to grief on the muddy minor roads that engulfed 12th SS Panzer in a sea of slime. Already for Sepp Dietrich the moment had passed by. The southern approach to Malmédy had now been completely blocked by the arrival of the US 1st Infantry Division. With the departure of 12th SS Panzer, the position of 2nd Division was greatly eased as it pulled back to Eisenborn Ridge. By 20 December the Americans were solidly entrenched in their new positions in the area.

Above: Eisenhower responded to the German offensive by ordering up any available reserves. Here glider infantry from the 82nd Airborne march towards the front line. Both the 82nd and 101st Airborne Divisions would add to their reputations in the Ardennes.

Along the American front there were significant reinforcements. The southern flank was bolstered with units of 1st Division, and 9th Division, having arrived from Aachen, had dug-in on the northern flank. There was now a strong defence line extending from Monschau in the north to Bullingen in the south and Waimes in the west. It was to withstand another concerted attempt to break through on 20 December. By then it had become abundantly clear that Dietrich's bludgeoning tactics would not dislodge the Americans from Eisenborn Ridge. In the northern sector of the Ardennes Front the only penetration – and that a narrow one – had been made by *Kampfgruppe* Peiper. The inexperienced men of 2nd and 99th Divisions had fatally unhinged the German offensive. Hitler's hopes now hung entirely on the actions of the 5th Panzer Army.

On the morning of 16 December 1944, General Dwight D. Eisenhower was in festive mood. He had just received a fifth star, becoming General of the Army, and General Omar Bradley was due to arrive at SHAEF headquarters in Versailles to discuss the

growing Allied manpower shortage, play bridge and, Eisenhower anticipated, share a meal of oysters. Roosevelt's press secretary, Steve Earley, had sent Eisenhower a bushel and he planned a veritable surfeit of oysters: oysters on the half-shell followed by oyster stew and then fried oysters. Before Bradley arrived, the Supreme Commander attended the wedding of his orderly, Sergeant Michael J. 'Mickey' McKeogh. There was to be no oyster feast for Bradley, however. The commander of 12th Army Group was allergic to them and was to dine off a meal of scrambled egg that night.

When Bradley arrived, Eisenhower immediately took him to a briefing room to discuss the growing manpower shortage in the Allied forces. However, their discussion was interrupted by a colonel from SHAEF's G-2 Section, who informed them that the Germans were attacking in the Ardennes in the sector held by VIII Corps. The colonel continued that reports were as yet fragmentary but the American line had been penetrated at several points and a threat was developing in the Losheim Gap.

Right: German motorcycle combinations in deep snow, evoking the words of Sepp Dietrich: 'All Hitler wants me to do is to cross a river, capture Brussels and then go on and take Antwerp! And all this in the worst time of year through the Ardennes where the snow is waist deep ...'

As Eisenhower's G-2, Major-General Strong outlined the points of German attack on the situation map. Bradley was calm, surmising that the Germans were launching a spoiling attack to dislocate 1st Army's attack on the Roer dams and 3rd Army's planned attack south of the Ardennes in the Saar. Within minutes, another message arrived indicating that eight German divisions not been previously identified in the Ardennes sector were involved in the attack. Eisenhower, maybe informed of the 'Magic' intercepts of Japanese diplomatic traffic, sensed danger, telling Bradley 'That's no spoiling attack.'

Eisenhower insisted that General Middleton's VIII Corps be sent some help. But there were only four uncommitted American divisions on the Western Front: 82nd and 101st Airborne, the European theatre reserve, were resting and re-fitting near Rheims after the failure of 'Market Garden'; 7th Armored was with 9th Army in Holland; and 10th Armored was in Patton's reserve south of the Ardennes.

Below: Men of the 1st Army manhandle an antitank gun into position to repel a German attack. The mud and snow affected both sides, causing difficulty in movement and a constriction on moving supplies or reinforcements up to the front line.

Eisenhower suggested sending the two armoured divisions to the Ardennes. When Bradley interjected that Patton, preparing his offensive in the Saar, would not be best pleased with relinquishing 10th Armored, Eisenhower barked, 'Tell him that Ike is running this damn war!' Indeed, when Bradley spoke to Patton on the telephone, the commander of 3rd Army was reluctant, to say the least, to release 10th Armored. Bradley told him, 'I've got to have that division, even if it's only a spoiling attack.' He then telephoned his staff in Luxembourg City with instructions to tell General Simpson to get 7th Armored on the road. He also advised Patton and Simpson to alert any other divisions that were out of the line to a possible move to the Ardennes.

Eisenhower had his oysters later that night in his handsome stone villa in St Germain-en-Laye, which had not long before been occupied by Field Marshal von Rundstedt. He cracked open a bottle of champagne with Bradley to celebrate his promotion and afterwards the two generals played a few rubbers of bridge. Shortly before they retired, at 23:00 hours, they were handed an 'Ultra' decrypt ordering *Luftwaffe* units in the Netherlands to be ready, on the morning of the 17th, to 'support the attack of 5th

and 6th Armies'. Both leaders went to their beds in thoughtful mood.

How was it that hard information from the Ardennes was taking so long to impact upon the Supreme Commander? Part of the problem lay with the long chain of command stretching from the front line back to Versailles. Disruption after the initial German bombardment clearly muddied the picture, but much of the information that did pass back up the line was stuck at the many filtering points where decisions had to be made about the relative significance of each item. Eisenhower and Bradley both compounded the problem by not talking directly to General Courtney Hodges, commander of 1st Army, and the man at the eye of the storm. Hodges had read Rundstedt's field order early on the afternoon of 16 January, and it had been forwarded immediately to the headquarters of 12th Army Group, where it had stopped. It was not until the morning of 17 January that Eisenhower and Bradley were also to read the order, and then via an 'Ultra' intercept.

Nevertheless, Eisenhower had set in motion the machinery to retrieve the situation in the Ardennes, although it would take at least 24 hours before the benefits could be perceived. The two American divisions in the south – 28th and 4th – were holding a 29km (18-mile) front with fewer than half their troops in the line. Throughout 16 December they fought hard against four infantry divisions of Brandenberger's 7th Army. At the northern edge of Brandenberger's sector, two of his infantry divisions, 5th Parachute and 352nd *Volksgrenadier*, cut off and isolated the most southerly of 28th Division's regiments. Further south, a single Combat Command of 9th Armored Division – brought into line to gain some experience – found itself locked in combat with 276th *Volksgrenadier* Division. At the southernmost end of 7th Army's assault zone 212th *Volksgrenadier* Division, a battle-hardened unit that had fought in Russia and consisted largely of Bavarian troops, had a tough struggle with a single regiment from 4th Division.

The regiment was 12th Infantry, and its paper strength was 3000. However, the quiet which had lapped the Ardennes Front before 16 December meant that many of 12th Infantry's men had been given passes to go to Luxembourg City and Paris. Only 5 of the Regiment's 12 companies were manning its outpost line in a string of picturesque villages on the western bank of the of the River Sure.

On the morning of 16 December, 212th *Volksgrenadier* crossed the Sure, overran 12th Regiment's forward outposts and surrounded its forward companies. But the men of the 12th did not panic. In Echternach, E Company – recently arrived

Above: American reinforcements on the march towards the front line of 1st Army. Despite a suitably festive scene, the Americans were in no mood to celebrate Christmas while the German offensive was threatening to break through their defences.

from the Hürtgen – turned a hat factory and the Hotel de Luxembourg into strongpoints blocking the main road towards Luxembourg City. In the neighbouring village of Berdorf, the plush Hotel Parc was occupied by men of F Company, commanded by Lieutenant John L. Leake. They were soon besieged by a strong enemy force. Other than their rifles, the men of B Company had only a few BARs, a machine gun and a small amount of reserve ammunition. Most of their reserve ammunition was in a small shed in the hotel garden which had now come under constant German fire.

At his headquarters in Luxembourg City, the commandeer of 4th Division, Major-General Raymond O. 'Tubby' Barton, radioed his five forward companies that there was to be 'no retrograde movement' in the sector held by 12th Regiment. At Echternach, the order was acknowledged but contact had been lost with Leake's company. To re-establish contact with the isolated company, the regimental commander, Colonel Robert H. Chance, sent B Company, reinforced by a platoon of light tanks and four mediums, to clear the village of Berdorf, which was strung out

Above: At the height of the Battle of the Bulge it seemed that the fighting was taking place in a giant refrigerator which turned the corpses of the fallen a deep scarlet. Many American units lacked suitable winter camouflage gear to hide them in the snow.

for 1km (0.6 miles) along a spine formed by the road from Consdorf, headquarters of the regiment's 2nd Battalion. The light tanks and half the infantrymen worked up the spine, house by house, while the rest of the men and the four medium tanks bypassed the village and approached the hotel.

To Leake's alarm the tanks manoeuvred to open fire. They had mistaken the Hotel Parc for a German strongpoint. Without his radio – it had been lost in the confused fighting of the 16th – Leake was unable to report his position; nor did he have any identification flares. As the tanks began shelling the hotel, one of Leake's men remembered that he had seen a Stars and Stripes flag in one of its rooms. It was raised from the roof but attracted heavy fire from German artillery on the eastern bank of the Sure.

Fierce fighting raged in and around Berdorf until 20 December. Lieutenant Leake and his men continued to hold the Hotel Parc. German artillery fire still plunged into the roof and rockets from *Panzerfausts* – hand-held recoilless antitank weapons – tore gaping holes in the walls. Maintaining constant watch at doors and windows, the American soldiers took a toll of any Germans unwise enough to show themselves in neighbouring houses. They sustained only one casualty, a soldier who was hit in the leg by a stray machine-gun bullet.

On the night of 19 December, Berdorf was blanketed in fog, enabling *Volksgrenadiers* to approach undetected to within 18m (20yd) of the hotel. Before dawn on the 20th, a huge blast rocked the east side of the hotel and the *Volksgrenadiers* attacked. In the murk, much of the fighting was with hand grenades. Dawn revealed that the explosion had exposed the hotel's superb wine cellar, but Leake and his men were not able to sample it. On the same day they received the order to withdraw from Berdorf, and clambered aboard tanks and halftracks in order to pull back 3km (2 miles) under the covering fire of 10th Armored Division's artillery.

In Echternach, E company had not been so lucky. By the morning of 19 December, Major-General Barton assumed that the men holding the hat factory would withdraw: he had sent a message to that effect with tanks of 10th Armored which had fought their way through to the factory, but somehow the message was not received. Nor did the officer commanding E Company, Lieutenant Morton A. Macdiarmid, take the opportunity to ask whether there had been a change in Barton's original order for 'no retrograde movement'. There was still a chance to pull the Americans out on the evening of the 19th, but the tank commander who might have rescued them was overly cautious about the strength of the German force in Echternach and reluctant to move around the town at night.

During the afternoon of the 20th, the American positions in the hat factory came under renewed and heavy attack by 212th *Volksgrenadiers*. As the American force which had held Echternach was withdrawing to a new defensive line, E Company was still holding the hat factory, and men of H Company the Hotel de Luxembourg. After being pounded by assault guns, 20 men of H Company and 110 of E Company surrendered, the victims of a tragic muddle over Major-General Barton's order to withdraw. It was small consolation to the exhausted men of 4th Division that the commander of 212th *Volksgrenadiers*, Major-General Franz Sensfuss, came to accept their surrender and inspect the small force that had given his formation so much trouble.

At the southern end of the Ardennes, 4th Division had been forced to yield ground but had nevertheless blunted the thrusts of Brandenberger's army for five days. In the north the single combat command of 9th Armored pulled back in good order to the southwest, limiting the German penetrations to 8km (5 miles). To the north, the isolated regiment of 28th Division, 12th Infantry, had fought off infiltrating *Volksgrenadiers* for two days while withdrawing over a tributary of the Sure, blowing the bridges behind it and eventually joining hands with 4th Division to the southeast. Together with 10th Armored Division and the recently arrived 5th Infantry Division, these units established a new defence line from the Echternach area in the east to the village of Grosbous in the west.

The battle in the south had been a confused affair but a signal American success. A solid line of defence had been formed which blocked any German hope of expansion to the south at the cost of some 2000 casualties. The shoulder in the south

had held, along with its counterpart in the north on the Eisenborn Ridge. The weight of the German offensive in the Ardennes was now channelled into the centre of its front along a significantly smaller road network than had been originally been contemplated. In turn, in this new and narrow attack corridor, the German vulnerability to American blocking action had been crucially increased.

With Brandenberger's army stalled in the south, and Dietrich's army in the north diverted from the direct northward route to Antwerp and forced due east, it was left to 5th Panzer Army to develop the main attack in the centre. Its commander, Hasso von Manteuffel, had originally been assigned a secondary role in 'Autumn Mist', attacking to the south of Dietrich, breaking through the American line and racing to the Meuse. Once the Meuse had been crossed, 5th Panzer Army was to strike northwest in order to shield the southern flank of 6th Panzer Army while it completed the operation's objective,

Below: A German soldier takes a pensive drag on his cigarette while his companion slumps exhausted against a tree stump. At key moments the German advance was halted by fatigue, compounding the slippage behind schedule which had occurred as soon as 'Autumn Mist' began.

the capture of Antwerp. Now, any hope of success rested with Manteuffel.

The initial headway made by Manteuffel was in large measure the result of the tactical modifications he had persuaded Hitler to adopt at their meeting shortly before the launching of Operation 'Autumn Mist'. Manteuffel used these vital concessions to further refine the opening assault in order to achieve the maximum impact. Small units were to be sent forwards to infiltrate the positions in the enemy's front line before the German artillery opened up. Handpicked 'storm battalions' were to bypass American positions to penetrate deep into the rear before the enemy had regained his balance. Along the greater part of Manteuffel's 45km (28-mile) front, his armour would not go into action until darkness

Below: A temporary position made of snow in the woods provides some shelter for these two German infantrymen belonging to one of Manteuffel's infantry divisions. Hand-picked men were to infiltrate the enemy lines before the main attack to cause maximum confusion.

had fallen on the night of 16 December. Its navigational aid would be 'artificial moonlight', searchlights reflected off low clouds.

The opening day of the offensive had seen Manteuffel's armour over the River Our, poised to press on to Clervaux. Now Manteuffel's main thrust was to hit the sector held by 110th Regiment along a 24km (15-mile) front, against which were to be thrown three divisions of General von Luttwitz's XXXXVII Panzer Corps, including the 2nd Panzer Division and also the *Panzer Lehr* Division.

The commander of 110th Regiment was Colonel Hurley E. Fuller, a veteran of the bitter World War I battle of the Argonne with a well-earned reputation as a curmudgeon. His regimental headquarters was located in the Hotel Claravallis in Clervaux, a picturesque town situated on a bend of the River Clerve at the meeting point of four steep gorges, dominated on its eastern edge by a 12th-century castle. Hurley's regiment had fought in the battle for the Hürtgen and had taken heavy casualties – mostly riflemen

and machine gunners – and had received some 2000 replacements for these losses. Assuming that the Ardennes Front would remain quiet, Hurley had planned to rotate his reserve battalion from time to time with the forward battalion. These plans were about to be set aside. Manteuffel needed the bridges on the River Clerve to press on to a high plateau which led to Highway N-12 and Bastogne.

Early in the morning of 16 December, Hurley's telephone lines were cut by the opening German bombardment. His radio wavelengths were jammed, and he was forced to piece together the unfolding drama of 'Autumn Mist' from a patchwork of fragmentary reports and rumours. Gradually, a picture was formed. The Germans had managed to break through his two forward battalions on Skyline Drive and were now driving westwards.

Fuller's original plan was to counterattack in battalion strength on Skyline Drive early on 17 December, but this tactic was overtaken by the speed of the German advance. The first crisis of the 17th arrived at about 09:30 hours when MkIVs and halftracks were spotted descending the steep, winding road to Clervaux from the direction of Marnach.

Above: A German Hummel *(Bumble Bee) self-propelled 150mm (5.9in) howitzer, carried on a MkIV panzer chassis. It was manned by a crew of six and from 1943 was to equip the six-gun heavy battery of a Panzer division's artillery regiment, but only 660 were made.*

Fuller despatched five Shermans of 707th Tank Battalion to meet them. The Germans were halted in a blaze of fire which accounted for four MkIVs. Another MkIV was disabled on the eastern approach to Clervaux by medium tanks commanded by First Lieutenant Raymond E. Fleig, blocking entry to German armour from this direction. However, by now Fuller's defences were being picked apart. The castle where his headquarters company was billeted had come under fire; and a scratch battalion composed of troops on leave in Clervaux, which Fuller had sent up the Marnach road, was straggling dispiritedly back into the town.

From mid-morning, Fuller had been putting through increasingly desperate telephone calls to his divisional commander, Major-General Norman D. 'Dutch' Cota, whose headquarters were in the town of Wiltz, some 16km (10 miles) southwest of Clervaux. One call secured a self-propelled tank

Above: American infantrymen shelter in a forest foxhole. Shellbursts among the trees were twice as deadly in forests as they were out in the open, sending showers of huge wooden splinters slicing into any infantry who had not yet taken cover.

destroyer platoon from 9th Armored's Combat Command R. It was sent up the road to Marnach to engage German tanks that were firing into the town. Shortly afterwards the vehicles came racing back at such speed that one of them overturned at a hairpin bend. The crew were pulled aboard one of the tank destroyers, which then motored off at top speed, never to be seen again.

Cota had instructed Fuller that he must 'hold at all costs'. His repeated requests to withdraw to a new position behind the Clerve, to block the road through St Vith to Bastogne, fell on deaf ears. By mid-afternoon the armoured ring around Clervaux had almost snapped shut. The tanks of 2nd Panzer Division were driving in from the western end of the town, and were now fast approaching Fuller's headquarters in the Hotel Claravallis.

At around 18:45 hours, Fuller was on the telephone again. This time he was speaking to Cota's chief of staff, Colonel Jesse L. Gibney. Once again Gibney refused to give permission to withdraw. As the two men were talking, Fuller was told that six German tanks were approaching his headquarters, information that Fuller passed on to Gibney with the observation that, as a Texan, he knew full well that he was being assigned the same fate as that which had befallen the defenders of the Alamo.

Despite Gibney's instruction, Fuller abandoned his headquarters. He emerged into a Clervaux which was, it seemed to him, ablaze from end to end, the flames cut by oily smoke and stabbed by German searchlights probing for targets. Through the streets nosed German tanks, pausing occasionally to pour fire into buildings which sheltered American troops. Fuller himself was soon taken prisoner as he attempted to rally some stragglers. A sergeant of 4th Division who knew him laconically remarked of Colonel Fuller's capture, 'The Krauts will sure be sorry they took Hurley.'

The bridges at Clervaux were not the only crossings of the Clerve seized by 5th Panzer Army. By noon on 18 December all the bridges south of the town were in German hands. Manteuffel could drive on to Bastogne, but was now 24 hours behind the unforgiving schedule of 'Autumn Mist'. On the same day, blocks on the main Clervaux–Bastogne road placed by VIII Corps were brushed aside by 5th Panzer Army. A new perimeter defence was hastily organized around Bastogne itself.

Major-General Cota now concentrated on defending his divisional headquarters at Wiltz, a road hub 16km (10 miles) southeast of Bastogne. The wisdom of this decision was debatable, as the defence of Wiltz would leave the main road from Ettelbruck to Bastogne wide open for German armour. Moreover, 5th Army already controlled the roads to Bastogne running north of Wiltz, the defence of which was now pointless. Nevertheless, Colonel Daniel B. Strickler, executive officer of 110th Regiment, deployed another makeshift force – drivers, clerks and bandsmen from divisional headquarters plus

Above: American reinforcements march past an M4 Sherman which is wearing camouflage to break up its outline. The Sherman was the mainstay of the American and British armoured divisions in northwest Europe and served in every major theatre of war.

some armour and a battalion of artillery – to hold Wiltz. By the evening of 19 December, it was clear that Strickler's position was hopeless. He told his unit commanders to fight their way out and make for Sibret, 2.5km (4 miles) southwest of Bastogne, where Cota planned to establish his divisional HQ.

Strickler stayed until 23:00 hours, destroying maps and papers before setting off in a jeep with a staff officer and a driver. Heavy artillery fire forced the small party to abandon the jeep west of Wiltz, and Strickler and his companions joined thousands of American troops straggling west through a wintry landscape, hiding up by day in forests and dodging German armour and patrols by night. It took them three days and three nights to gain the safety of the village of Vaux-les-Rosières, the newly established headquarters of 28th Division.

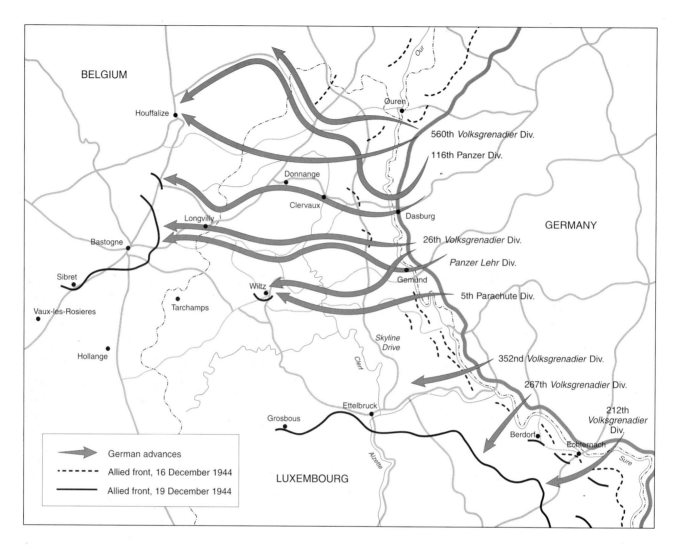

Above: German armoured fingers grope for Bastogne, the vital road centre whose capture Hitler had ordered at all costs. Its importance derived from the fact that from Bastogne extended roads that took in all the principal elements of the Ardennes roadnet.

Cota's division had taken a drubbing but had lived to fight another day. A harsher fate was to overtake 106th Infantry Division. In common with divisions that had not gone overseas before US battlefield casualties began to mount, 106th had been forced to yield up many of its trained troops as replacements for formations fighting in northern Europe. In 1944 it lost over 7000 men, 60 per cent of its enlisted strength. Shortly before it embarked for Europe, 106th received 1200 men from the Army Specialized Training Programme (ASTP), 1100 who had been training as air cadets, 1500 from divisions not yet scheduled to go overseas, and 2500 men from disbanded units. It had been a debilitating process although not unique to 106th Division, which had been brought back to full strength, but without time to develop the ésprit de corps essential to combat.

The division had arrived early in December and had established headquarters at St Vith, 24km (15 miles) behind the front line. Two of its three regiments went forward to hold the Schnee Eifel, the ridge jutting into Germany's West Wall defences. In the north, 422nd Regiment occupied positions on a 6.5km (4-mile) front along the crest and eastern slopes of the Schnee Eifel; in the centre 423rd Regiment held a frontage of about 8km (5 miles) with a single battalion positioned on the southern edge of the Schnee Eifel opposite the village of Bleialf. The third regiment, 424th, was separated from 423rd by the valley of the River Alf and was deployed along a 9.5km (6-mile) frontage on the south of 106th's sector.

The commander of 106th Division, Major-General Alan W. Jones, had the deepest misgivings about the positions of these regiments. With the River Our at its back, 424th Regiment had little room to manoeuvre if it was attacked. The two regiments on the Schnee Eifel were even more exposed. In their rear, the road network gave an enemy attacking around

THE BATTLE FOR EISENBORN RIDGE

either or both ends of the Schnee Eifel an opportunity for two envelopments. From the village of Auw, in the Losheim Gap, a road ran south along a ridge – Skyline Boulevard – which would enable a shallow envelopment. From Andler, in the Losheim Gap, a road followed the River Our to link at Schoenberg, 13km (8 miles) due east of St Vith, with a road from Bleialf to offer a deeper envelopment.

Major-General Jones' fears were not groundless. On 16 December two regiments of 18 *Volksgrenadiers*, a formation which had enjoyed two months' experience in the Eifel, brushed aside 14th Cavalry Group in the Losheim Gap, and by noon was threatening the northern flank of 422nd

Regiment. A *Volksgrenadier* battalion headed for Auw, which was held by a company of 81st Engineer Combat Battalion, 106th Division's organic engineers. Under heavy fire from German assault guns of the *Führer Begleit* brigade, the engineers' withdrawal was covered by Corporal Edward S. Withee who distracted the German gunners and survived to be taken prisoner as the village fell into German hands. The way to Schoenberg lay open.

Below: Within a forest, a German tank crew pauses for reflection at night in front of a welcome fire. Even as the offensive reached its height, the thoughts of men on both sides were turning towards Christmas and their families waiting for them at home.

Above: American reinforcements move up to counter the German threat to St Vith. Like Bastogne, St Vith was an important crossroads on the road network in this part of the Ardennes, and control of the town would allow the Germans to move their forces with greater ease.

At the southern end of the Schnee Eifel, a regiment of 18th *Volksgrenadier* Division pushed up the valley of the River Alf to overrun the positions held by 423rd Regiment's antitank company and capture the greater part of Bleialf. Later that day the village was retaken by an improvised force of engineers and headquarters troops, but this success only delayed the German drive. As the southern pincer of 18th *Volksgrenadier* swung around the bottom end of the Schnee Eifel, the exposed American regiments were menaced from two directions. The gap between the closing pincers, which was now no more than 8km (5 miles) wide, was fast narrowing.

To the south, 424th Regiment's position in Winterspelt was under the partial control of 62nd *Volksgrenadier* Division. St Vith – only 9.5km (6 miles) to the northwest – was now under threat. Remaining in constant contact with General

Left: German mortar crews get ready to move out. The German Army used 50mm (1.9in), 81mm (3.1in) and 120mm (4.7in) weapons which were manned by infantry to provide covering fire or to deliver smoke in order to conceal movement.

Middleton, commander of VIII Corps, Major-General Jones strove to exercise a grip on the battle which was now developing behind the Schnee Eifel. Middleton had placed Combat Command B of 9th Armored Division at his disposal, but as its armour was stationed 19km (12 miles) north of St Vith, no help could be expected from this quarter until the next day. Jones' own efforts to move up the reserve battalion of 423rd Regiment descended into chaos, and these troops spent the 16th on a mystery tour of the countryside around Schoenberg and therefore played no part in that day's fighting.

As night fell, 424th Regiment had been pinned back on the River Our and 422nd and 423rd were threatened with total encirclement by 18th *Volksgrenadiers*. In St Vith, General Middleton conferred with Major-General Jones and suggested that the two regiments on the Schnee Eifel be pulled

back. He later said that he had the gravest reservations about this, fearing that once they began to withdraw, the two inexperienced regiments might not stop withdrawing until they had got halfway back to Paris.

Jones, the man on the spot, decided to leave the regiments in place. Influencing his decision was a reassurance from Middleton that a combat command from 7th Armored Division would be rushed into Jones' sector by 07:00 hours the next morning, at the same time as Combat Command B of 9th Armored Division. But the tanks of 7th Armored were over 110km (70 miles) away and neither Middleton nor Jones – two experienced officers – queried the unrealistic assumption that their entire column would cover the distance in so short a time. With Jones when he received the news about the 7th Division armour was the assistant G-2 of VIII Corps, Lieutenant-Colonel William H. Slayden, who immediately grasped the over-optimistic view of the arrival of the combat command. But Slayden said nothing, reasoning that on this occasion it was not his place, as a junior officer, to speak up against the commander's decision. As he was later to observe, 'That would have put me in the position of calling the corps commander a liar.'

Jones had been dealt a tough hand. He had climbed the Army's greasy pole in peacetime and now, on his first day of combat, he was staring disaster in the face. Moreover, his son was serving as a lieutenant with a battalion of 423rd Regiment, and Jones was fearful that any order from him to retreat might be interpreted as a device to save his son. So Jones placed his faith in the arrival of the reinforcing armour. The tanks from 9th Armored would go to the aid of 424th Regiment; those of 7th Armored would be rushed to the Schnee Eifel.

The tanks did not arrive, and the German envelopment of the American forces on the Schnee Eifel was completed when, at 08:30 hours, the northern and southern arms of the pincer met at Schoenberg. As morning became afternoon, the American armour was still on the road, its advance elements snarled up in a colossal traffic jam west of St Vith. At 14:45 hours, Major-General Jones radioed his ensnared

regiments to fall back to the west bank of the Our, but the message – swamped by traffic – did not get through until after midnight. However, it was superseded by another order, received at 02:25 hours, ordering 422nd and 423rd Regiments to attack concentrations of enemy armour between Schoenberg and St Vith and then move into positions defending St Vith from attack from the east. They were to be sustained by airdrops; food, ammunition and medical supplies were now running dangerously low.

Like the armour, the airdrops never materialized. Nevertheless, the attacks on Schoenberg went in on the morning of 19 December after nightmarish approach marches over murderously muddy terrain blanketed by fog. As the commander of 422nd Regiment, Colonel George L. Descheneaux, had feared when he originally received his orders, the men of the two regiments were cut to pieces in conditions of murderous confusion. At one point in the battle a firefight broke out between units of the two regiments. German tanks and antiaircraft guns fired on them and finished the job. Descheneaux called together his battalion commanders, told them that 'We're sitting like fish in a pond' and, with tears in his eyes, announced his intention to surrender. He had decided to save as many of his men's lives as he was able and did not care if this eventually led to a court martial. The commander of 423rd Infantry, Colonel Charles C. Cavender, had reached the same conclusion, and at 16:00 hours he surrendered. Among Cavender's men taken prisoner was the son of the divisional commander, Major-General Jones.

A last stand was made by some 500 men of 422nd who rallied on nearby rising ground and dug in with halftracks of 634th Antiaircraft Artillery Battalion. However, they came under intense heavy bombardment the next day and so agreed to surrender early on the morning of 21 December. This brought an end to the most costly defeat suffered by the US Army in Europe. During the fighting in the Schnee Eifel, 422nd and 423rd Infantry Regiments, along with their attached and supporting units, had lost more than 8000 men, some 3000 of whom had surrendered in the late afternoon of 19 December.

The remaining regiment of 106th Division, 424th, was driven out of Winterspelt on 17 December and withdrew across the Our, where they joined hands with the tanks of Combat Command B of 9th Armored Division. The division had been ordered to abandon its attempt to retake Winterspelt, which had become but a pointless exercise in the light of the crisis on the Schnee Eifel. A new front line was assembled on the west bank of the Our – stiffened by advanced elements of 7th Armored Division – to block the path to St Vith.

CHAPTER SIX

The Americans Rally

There will only be cheerful faces at this conference table.

General Eisenhower, 19 December 1944

By 19 December, three days after the start of 'Autumn Mist', American strength in the Ardennes sector had doubled from 90,000 to 180,000. On 16 December there had been one armoured and five infantry divisions; now there were three armoured and ten infantry (including two airborne) divisions, and another division, 3rd Armored, was arriving. The Germans had committed 4 panzer and 13 parachute and *Volksgrenadier* divisions, and the *Führer Begleit* brigade was moving on St Vith. Sepp Dietrich retained two uncommitted SS panzer divisions, and Model at Army Group B had a reserve of a panzer, Panzergrenadier and a *Volksgrenadier* division. Beyond that lay the so-called *Führer* reserve, two of whose divisions, the 9th Panzer and the 15th *Volksgrenadier*, had been earmarked for possible use in 15th Army's projected attack in the Aachen sector.

On the northern and southern shoulders of the salient, the Americans were holding, respectively, 6th and 7th Armies. In the centre, however, the situation remained fluid and potentially dangerous. *Kampfgruppe* Peiper had driven deep behind American lines, and between St Vith and Bastogne two panzer divisions of von Manteuffel's 5th Panzer

Left: Gently does it. Some 47,500 US servicemen were wounded in six weeks of fighting in the Ardennes; the medical services were pushed to the limit. Stretcher bearers took wounded men through hip-deep snow-drifts and along icy road, improvising sleds to get them to aid stations.

Army – 2nd and 116th – had surged forward to reach the north–south highway connecting Bastogne through Houffalize to Liège. There were, at present, only scattered American units in this sector to oppose a continued thrust by these two divisions to the Meuse. Continuing poor weather was still preventing the application of pressure by Allied air power. During the opening days of 'Autumn Mist', tactical aircraft had managed only a few sorties. Among them had been a strafing and bombing attack on *Kampfgruppe* Peiper on 18 December. The attack had caused little damage but had nevertheless slowed the progress of Peiper's column.

Eisenhower was now receiving a stream of 'Ultra' decrypts that identified most of the 17 divisions so far committed to Operation 'Autumn Mist'. Linked to the decrypt of von Rundstedt's hortatory order to the troops, it painted a picture of an operation of significantly greater scale than a spoiling attack. On 19 December the Supreme Commander met with his top field commanders and the key members of their staffs at 12th Army Group's headquarters in Verdun. Present at the meeting were Bradley, Patton and General Jacob Devers, the commander of 6th Army Group, as well as Eisenhower's deputy, Air Chief Marshal Sir Arthur Tedder.

Eisenhower set the mood of the conference by telling his attentive colleagues: 'The present situation is to be regarded as one of opportunity for us and not of disaster. There will only be cheerful faces at

Above: No time to lose. Shouting orders and pointing the way, a German officer hurries his men past a disabled American halftrack. Any working American vehicles would have been captured and used by the Germans against their Allied enemy.

the conference table.' He went on to say that all offensive action was to cease. There was to be no withdrawal beyond the Meuse. Devers was to shift 6th Army Group's boundary north in order to free some of Patton's 3rd Army for a drive into the southern German flank. Meanwhile Simpson's 9th Army was to perform the same function for Hodges' 1st Army. In Eisenhower's view, Hodges was too preoccupied with the containment of German thrusts to contemplate an immediate counterattack in the north. It would be left to Patton to drive to Bastogne before linking up with the forces of 1st Army.

Eisenhower then turned to Patton and asked him when he could start. This was the moment for which the showman commander of 3rd Army had been waiting. He shot back, 'On 21 December, with three divisions.' There was consternation. Patton was proposing to pull three divisions out of the line and

wheel them north in the space of three days, a manoeuvre of the utmost complexity. Taken aback, Eisenhower cautioned Patton not to be fatuous. Chewing a fat cigar, Patton relished the moment. He explained that he had already drawn up three plans to meet the crisis. He had only to telephone his chief of staff, one Brigadier-General Hobart R. Gay, and give him the codeword to activate the plan that called for a drive on Bastogne.

That night Eisenhower faced another decision. It was clear that the expanding German salient was threatening to sever Bradley's communications with his troops on the northern side of the 'bulge' swelling in the Allied line. Bradley evinced no desire to move his headquarters from Luxembourg City, in the southeast of the Ardennes theatre, and thus could not exercise close personal control over 1st Army's critical sector in the north. If all the Allied troops north of this penetration were to become involved in the fighting, then Eisenhower needed a single commander to control the four armies located there. The senior field commander closest to the threat in the north was Field Marshal Montgomery,

Left: General Patton (left), seen here talking to Brigadier-General McAuliffe after the relief of Bastogne, was ordered to swing his 3rd Army through 90 degrees and attack the flank of the German thrust. Patton had anticipated such a request, and was ready to comply.

whose 21st Army Group possessed the only substantial reserve then available on continental Europe: this was the British XXX Corps.

Eisenhower's G-2, Major-General Strong, then made a suggestion: that Bradley's command be split. In the north, Montgomery would take temporary control of the 1st and 9th Armies, while at the same time, Bradley would remain in charge of VIII Corps as well as Patton's 3rd Army in the south. However, the practical solution to the pressing problem in the Ardennes carried with it a significant potential for political trouble within the Allied High Command

Below: A map showing the entirety of the German drive towards Antwerp, the dislocation of Bradley's communications with 1st and 9th Armies, and the position of the British reserve, XXX Corps. Also visible are the defensive positions around St Vith and Bastogne.

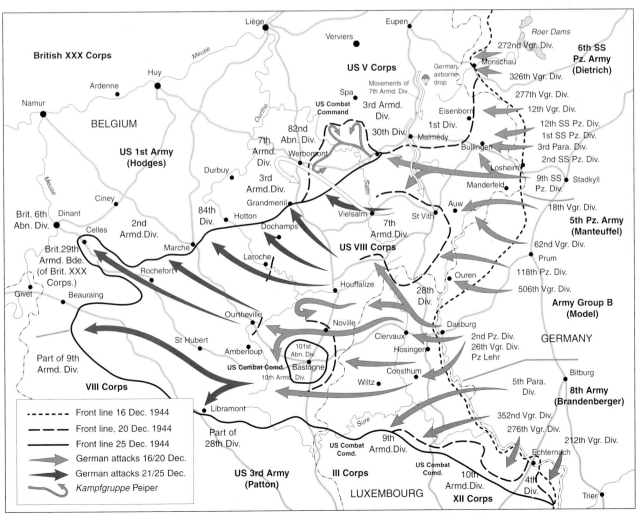

itself. Such a move could be seen as a slight to Bradley, and could also prompt the abrasive Montgomery to revive his campaign to be placed in overall command of the land battle in northern Europe, which he had pursued from the outset.

Nevertheless, Eisenhower realized that the proposal made for tighter battle control and might also encourage Montgomery to commit British reserves to the battle. Inevitably, Bradley was upset by the decision when he was informed on the telephone by Bedell Smith. At first he accused Supreme Headquarters Allied Expeditionary Force (SHAEF) staff of succumbing to panic, but even he had to admit that the proposal represented the only logical course of action, even if Montgomery's assumption of control over his own beloved 1st Army stuck in Bradley's craw. Nor was Patton overly impressed

with the decision, which he ascribed to the psychological domination that Montgomery exerted over the Supreme Commander. Patton concluded from the outcome of the meeting that Ike was 'unwilling or unable to command Montgomery'.

With his sublime lack of tact, Montgomery could not resist the opportunity to 'tweak our Yankee noses', as Bradley tartly put it. As one of the Field Marshal's staff officers recalled, Montgomery arrived at the headquarters of 1st Army 'like Christ come to cleanse the temple'. He declined to consult a detailed map which had been prepared for him by Hodges' operations staff, but instead insisted on consulting a smaller version prepared by his own 'Phantom' officers who had been visiting the front for several days. He turned down an offer to lunch with Hodges, eating a picnic by himself; this was his customary ritual, but in the circumstances became a gesture calculated to unsettle his American allies.

Despite this tension, Eisenhower's move had the desired effect. Montgomery despatched elements of XXX Corps to support the tank units already sent to

Below: Field Marshal Montgomery and Lieutenant-General William H. 'Big Bill' Simpson, commander of US 9th Army, on the Siegfried Line. Simpson and the commander of 1st Army, Courtney Hodges, were temporarily placed under Monty's command by Eisenhower.

guard the bridges over the Meuse. Montgomery's instincts prompted him to suggest to the Americans that they withdraw from exposed positions, like that in St Vith, to 'tidy up the battlefield'. However, when this suggestion was hotly contested, Monty had the good sense not to press the point. The Americans were determined to make a stand at St Vith; like their German counterparts they considered it one of the keys to the struggle in the northern sector of the 'bulge'. Possession of the town meant control of six paved highways. By 20 December, panzers had swept past St Vith to the north and south, but their attenuated spearheads were now threatened by the Americans in St Vith, whose presence prevented the efficient resupply of their forward elements.

The formation with the principal responsibility for defending St Vith was 7th Armored Division. The division had originally been promised as a reinforcement for the beleaguered regiments of 106th Division on the Schnee Eifel. When the commander of 7th Armored, Brigadier-General Robert W. Hasbrouck, had received the order to move, his division was in the southern-most part of the Netherlands, 97km (60 miles) from St Vith. It was not until dawn on the following day that

Above: Troops of Montgomery's British XXX Corps, the only significant Allied reserve in Europe in December 1944, move through winter murk. The soldier on the left is armed with a Sten gun, a submachine gun of extremely simple construction, and cheap to manufacture.

the first of Hasbrouck's vehicles got underway. Thus, even with the most favourable conditions, it would be well into the day before any substantial elements could reach St Vith before pushing on to Schoenberg to open up an escape corridor for 106th Regiment. Planning and deployment for the planned attack would consume yet more precious time.

At 11:00 hours on 17 December, the leading element of 7th Armored, Combat Command B, reached the Belgian town of Vielsalm, paused to refuel and then swung east to St Vith. Immediately it ran into a massive traffic jam heading westward. An officer of the division's 38th Armored Infantry Battalion, Major Donald P. Boyer, described it as 'a constant stream of traffic hurtling to the rear [to the west] and nothing going to the front [to the east]. We realized that this was not a convoy moving to the rear; it was a case of "every dog for himself"; it was a retreat, a rout.' In fact, this mass of traffic – trucks, artillery prime

121

movers, jeeps – was heading west under orders, although this did nothing to ease the chaos. The lead vehicles of 7th Armored's column stuck fast at the village of Poteau. It took General Hasbrouck five hours to negotiate the 18km (11 miles) from Vielsalm to St Vith. There he called a halt. The fate of the two trapped regiments of 106th Division was sealed. It would have been small consolation to Hasbrouck had he known that the mirror-image of this chaos was to be found on the German side of the front, where Manteuffel found himself trapped in a massive snarl-up on the way to Schoenberg where he had intended to spend the night at the headquarters of 18th *Volksgrenadier* Division. He was reduced to walking, as was the commander of Army Group B, Field Marshal Model. The two commanders bumped into each other and exchanged words. Manteuffel assured Model that St Vith would fall to 5th Panzer Army on 18 December.

Below: A German soldier poses by a captured US howitzer covered in a layer of snow. By this stage of the war the Germans were inclined to use any weapon available against the Allies, which suggests that the howitzer has either run out of ammunition, or has been put out of action.

By midnight on 17 December a defence line had been established around St Vith and strengthened with units from the front, among them the remaining regiment of 106th Division and a combat command of 9th Armored Division. The following morning the defences came under probing attack from 18th *Volksgrenadier* Division, striking at four separate positions on the 24km (15-mile) horseshoe-shaped perimeter. The line held, and on 19 December the defenders of St Vith were boosted by the arrival from the southeast of the withdrawing 112th Infantry Regiment, which had been separated from 28th Division. Widely spaced jabs delivered by 18th *Volksgrenadiers* continued for two more days, but became increasingly ineffectual. The severe traffic problems that Manteuffel was experiencing were preventing him from landing a knockout blow. The stern American resistance on the Eisenborn Ridge had shuffled the German drive to the south, tangling units of 6th and 5th Panzer Armies as the schedule for 'Autumn Mist' slipped back yet further.

By the evening of 20 December, Manteuffel had grown weary of the stalemate at St Vith. The continued American hold on the road hub was dislocating 5th

Above: A jumble of German transports on an icy road. The problem faced by the Germans in the execution of 'Autumn Mist' was the allocation of sufficient fuel to cross the Meuse and race for Antwerp. Once the Allied fighter-bombers operated at will, the question became academic.

Army's drive to the Meuse. The attack on the town was to be made by 18th *Volksgrenadier* Division and a regiment of 62nd *Volksgrenadier* Division. Because 18th *Volksgrenadiers* had problems reaching their start line, it was not until 15:00 hours that German artillery opened up with a heavy preliminary bombardment. As dusk was drawing in, shelling shifted from the American front line to command posts in the rear and to St Vith. The *Volksgrenadiers* moved forward, and as darkness fell small groups of Germans had broken through the American lines, killing messengers and engaging command posts.

At the apex of the horseshoe facing the eastern approaches to St Vith, six Tigers of 506th Heavy Panzer Battalion approached the road into St Vith running west from Schoenberg. Five Shermans of 31st Tank Battalion were ordered to take positions

Left: A Tiger of 2nd SS Panzer Division Das Reich *in the Ardennes in late December 1944. Massively armoured and relatively slow, the Tiger was a daunting sight when moving forward, machine guns blazing, but was all too prone to be left stranded in a fast-moving battle.*

Above: An American machine-gunner dug in ready to receive the enemy near St Vith. His position has been covered with a layer of snow, and a sheet helps camouflage his Browning machine gun. A bazooka lies nearby, ready for use in case a German Panzer attacks.

from which they could cover a rise in the road and, when the Tigers breasted it, fire simultaneously. As the Tigers crossed the rise, they fired a salvo of white flares that burst behind the American tanks with a brilliant white light, blinding the gunners and silhouetting the Shermans, which were destroyed one by one. The Tigers then switched their attention to American machine-gun crews blocking the road. The survivors of the attack broke for the rear.

Unnerved by the brutality of the German assault, the officer commanding the defences in front of St Vith, Lieutenant-Colonel William H.G. Fuller, headed for the headquarters of Brigadier-General Bruce C. Clarke, commander of 7th Division's Combat Command B to 'plan alternate positions'. When he arrived, Fuller told Clarke that he could take no more. Clarke put the agitated Fuller in the hands of doctors, who evacuated him.

The Tigers rumbled along the road into St Vith, from which a stream of vehicles was heading west,

American soldiers scrambling aboard. By midnight, Brigadier-General Clarke had formed a new line to the west of the town, and officers posted on roads and trails were halting stragglers and directing them to their positions. Fortunately for Clarke, the Germans were in no position to exploit the capture of St Vith. Most of the roads leading into the town converged in a bottleneck that produced another nightmarish traffic jam. Moreover, the men of 18th and 62nd *Volksgrenadiers* were eager to find booty and warmth, and in the frenzied scavenging units were hopelessly intermingled. Officers and men roared about in captured vehicles as elements of 6th Panzer Army, still searching for a way around the traffic stalled in the Losheim Gap, also entered St Vith. Such was the confusion that Field Marshal Model, arriving in St Vith five days behind schedule, was once again forced to get out and walk.

As the badly mauled American forces regrouped west of St Vith, Brigadier-General Hasbrouck, the commander of 7th Armored Division, received a message from Major-General Matthew B. Ridgway, commander of the recently arrived XVIII Corps, whose 82nd Airborne Division on the west bank of the River Salm, 16km (10 miles) west of St Vith had

*Right: Major-General Matthew B. Ridgway (left), commander of
XVIII Airborne Corps, who was later to lead the UN Command in
Korea, and Major-General James M. Gavin, commander of 82nd
Airborne Division and the youngest general in the US Army.*

made contact with patrols of 7th Armored Division.
At that moment command of all forces in the St Vith
sector passed to Ridgway who, with the airborne
soldier's sanguine attitude towards envelopment,
believed that troops beyond the Salm could hold. A
relatively firm line was being established by 82nd
Airborne, which Ridgway was confident would prevent the Germans from cutting the salient from the
rear; and an anticipated attack by 3rd Armored
Division might remove all threat of encirclement.

In the small hours of 22 December, Ridgway
ordered the forces in the St Vith salient to shorten
their lines by withdrawing into an oval-shaped
defensive position in front of and encompassing
Vielsalm. This was to be dubbed the 'goose egg', in

*Below: Men of the 505th Parachute Infantry Regiment, part of the
82nd Airborne Division, who were involved in the fighting around St
Vith. Neither the 82nd nor the 101st Airborne Divisions had much in
the way of antitank weapons.*

which the air-supplied defenders of the 'egg' were to await the arrival of 3rd Armored. To resolve the knotty problems of command that had accompanied the defence of and withdrawal from St Vith, Ridgway attached 7th Armored to 106th Division under the overall command of Major-General Jones.

Neither Hasbrouck nor his subordinate, Clarke, were impressed by the 'goose egg'. It would have an extensive perimeter and take in a thick forest outside Vielsalm. The roads looked impressive on a map, but with the exception of a single gravel highway cutting across the forest, they were dirt tracks. Moreover, the supply of troops in the egg depended on the area to the west of the forest being kept accessible by the airborne troops. And how could the armour be supplied effectively by air? Clarke dubbed Ridgway's plan 'Custer's Last Stand'. Even as the plan went forward, Hasbrouck was writing a report to Ridgway, pointing out that there was only one bridge at Vielsalm and that even that might be denied to the defenders of the 'goose egg' should 2nd SS Panzer Division, which was known to be south of the salient, drive the airborne

Below: German troops discuss the disposition of American prisoners. The soldier in the centre of the picture has slung a Panzerfaust *over his shoulder. During the Battle of the Bulge, many American prisoners were killed in cold blood as soon as they surrendered.*

troops back by two-thirds of a mile. He concluded his report with the frank observation: 'In my opinion if we don't get out of here before night, we will not have a 7th Armored left'.

Doubts began to assail Ridgway. He consulted Jones and Hasbrouck. The former seemed eerily detached and optimistic about the plan's chances of success; he was soon to be relieved of his command by Ridgway and suffer a massive heart attack. Hasbrouck reiterated his misgivings, emphasizing the exhaustion of the troops. Ridgway then went forward to look for himself and canvas more opinion, including that of Brigadier-General William H. Hoge, commander of 9th Armored's Combat Command B (CCB), a man of rock-solid imperturbability whom Ridgway knew well. Watching intently for Hoge's reaction, Ridgway informed Hoge that he would begin to withdraw that night: 'We're going to get you out of here.' Hoge's terse reply was 'How can you?' It was enough to convince Ridgway that he should withdraw. He told Hoge, 'Bill, we can and we will.'

By then, however, the decision had been taken out of Ridgway's hands. Montgomery ordered a withdrawal from the 'goose egg', adding a tribute to the defenders of St Vith: 'They can come back with all honour. They come back to more secure positions. They put up a wonderful show.' Of the 22,000

troops, 5000 had been killed, wounded or captured, and 7th Armored Division had lost 60 tanks.

The troops were to pull out on 23 December, through a narrow corridor held open by 82nd Airborne Division, but a sudden thaw had turned the roads into a morass in which stalled vehicles were sitting ducks for German artillery. Then, early in the morning of the 23rd, it froze again. At 06:00 hours Major-General Clarke gave the order to move. While a task force of 7th Armored Division covered the retreat, the defenders of St Vith crossed the Salm. At 20:30 hours, after four attempts and under fire from German armour, a small detachment of airborne engineers blew the road and rail bridges at Vielsalm.

Hasso von Manteuffel had counted on taking St Vith and its network of roads by the end of the first day of 'Autumn Mist'. He had reached the town at the end of the sixth day, 21 December. It was a critical delay that was to further unhinge 'Autumn Mist'. By the time the 'goose egg' collapsed, British tank units were guarding the Meuse bridges, while to the east of the river US VII Corps was readying itself for a counterattack. On the northern flank of the bulge,

US 30th Division had moved into a blocking position along the River Amblève in the Malmédy sector.

It was at Malmédy that men of *Kampfgruppe* Peiper had run amok. The deployment of 30th Division along the length of the Amblève was to lead to a showdown with Peiper's command, which was now pushing on down the valley of the river and leaving a trail of terror in its wake.

On 17 December *Kampfgruppe* Peiper had left the crossroads at Malmédy and driven south to the village of Ligneuville, a prewar haunt of tourists who came to see the wild boar in the forests nearby. Now it was the headquarters of Brigadier-General Timberlake, commander of 49th Antiaircraft Artillery Brigade, who was housed in the Hotel du Moulin at the northern edge of Ligneuville. Timberlake and his staff had made a hasty departure by the time Peiper rolled into Ligneuville, leaving behind a meal to

Below: Members of an SS division, riding in an amphibious vehicle, check a sign at a vital crossroads. The Battle of the Bulge hinged on the possession of key road junctions. The Germans needed to seize them and the Americans needed to deny them possession.

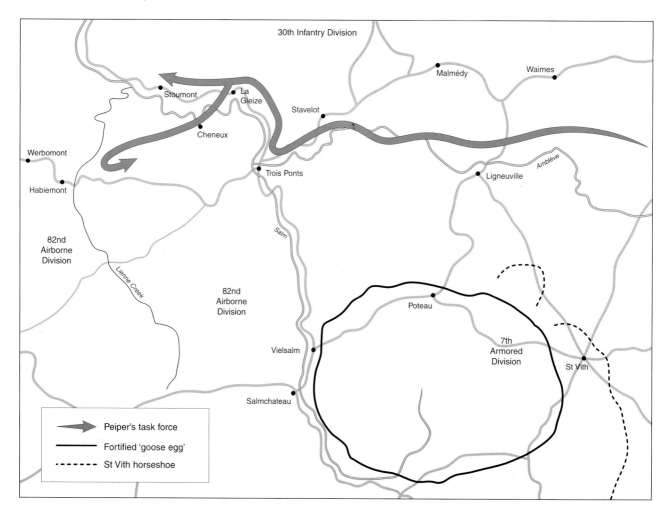

Above: A map showing the 'goose egg' near St Vith, and the furthest penetration of Kampfgruppe Peiper. By this stage Peiper's men had been on the move for the past three days, and were utterly exhausted and running out of fuel.

which Peiper helped himself. Meanwhile his troops rounded up a rearguard force of Americans. They were marched up Ligneuville's main street and eight of them were ordered by a German sergeant to dig graves for three dead German soldiers. Once they had finished, the sergeant lined them up in a row and shot them in the head, one by one. These grisly proceedings were witnessed by a Belgian farmer's wife, Madame Lochem.

The eighth man, Corporal Joseph P. Mass, would survive. During the afternoon he played dead and then, as darkness fell, he crawled to a nearby clump of trees. He was given food and directions by a Belgian civilian, but was later captured trying to make his way to St Vith. The 14 Americans who had survived owed their lives to the owner of the Hotel du Moulin, who plied their guards with wine and cognac and distracted them from carrying out an order from an SS officer to kill them all.

Peiper had left Ligneuville before the killing began. His column had pushed on to the River Amblève, reaching the heights that looked down on the village of Stavelot on the opposite bank. Here the winding road hugged the cliff until it was carried over the river on a stone bridge. Peiper's scouts reported that the streets of Stavelot were packed with traffic, their headlights blazing. Peiper had no way of telling that this was a gathering of supply trucks massing to pull out. They might be a substantial defence force. And *Kampfgruppe* Peiper had to push on to find an American fuel dump in order to sustain its drive on to the Meuse.

Unknown to Peiper, a squad from C Company, 291st Engineer Combat Battalion, commanded by Sergeant Charles Hensel, had established a roadblock on the road his armour was descending. At a sharp bend in the road they were laying mines covered by a bazooka and machine gun. Just ahead of the bend, Hensel had stationed a lookout, Private Bernard Goldstein. He had been there only a few minutes when he heard the approach of tracked vehicles moving slowly, and German voices. When the tanks were only a few metres away from him, he

Above: The crew of an M10 tank destroyer pose by their vehicle. They were responsible for knocking out four German Tigers in Stavelot. Expended shell cases from the vehicle's 76.2mm (3in) gun are strewn around as evidence of its recent use.

stepped out into the road, his M-1 carbine at the ready, and gave the order, 'Halt!'

Hensel, on his way up to Goldstein's position with another soldier, could hardly believe his ears. Then the night was split by fire from the tank's machine gun and the two men raced back around the bend. The tank loosed off a round at Goldstein, and the shell whistled past his head. Goldstein scampered up the hill above the road and escaped while Peiper's panzers rumbled on towards the bridge. As the lead tank crept around the bend, it was damaged by fire from Hensel's bazooka.

At that point the customarily hard-driving Peiper called a halt. He had decided that his tanks were too vulnerable on the narrow road into Stavelot and that he would delay his attempt to take the bridge. *Kampfgruppe* Peiper had been on the road for three days and three nights, and he and his men were exhausted and needed some rest. The accumulation of delays during the last 24 hours had ensured that Peiper had arrived at Stavelot in darkness, unable to distinguish between lorries moving out of the town

and reinforcements moving in. The slippage in 'Autumn Mist' was gradually becoming fatal.

Below Peiper, in Stavelot, the bridge was being prepared for demolition. But the engineers whose task it was – men of 202nd Engineer Combat Battalion – had been infiltrated by two of Skorzeny's commandos. They ensured that the bridge remained standing. At about 04:00 hours, as a company of 526th Armored Infantry Battalion was establishing positions on the east bank of the river, it came under attack from *Kampfgruppe* Peiper. The Armored Infantry Battalion's tank destroyers accounted for four of Peiper's tanks, but could not keep his column out of Stavelot. At 08:00 hours, 526th Battalion was withdrawn, falling back on the road to Malmédy. Peiper ordered the bulk of his column to swing west to his next objective, Trois Ponts, and left a detachment to mop up in Stavelot.

Here they resumed the killing: eight American prisoners of war were shot out of hand; a tank fired into a group of Belgian civilians, killing two and wounding two more; grenades were thrown into a cellar sheltering more civilians. At least 100 people were killed before the rage of *Kampfgruppe* Peiper subsided.

Major Paul Solis, the executive officer of 526th Battalion, had not withdrawn towards Malmédy but had driven towards Spa in a halftrack. His route took him to a large American fuel dump, containing 4.5 million litres (one million gallons) of petrol, just outside Stavelot. Most of the fuel, in 23-litre (5-gallon) jerrycans, was stored in the woods that lined the road, although some of it lay in the open. It was guarded by a platoon of 5th Fusilier Battalion, the first unit of the Belgian Army to be formed after that country's liberation, and filled principally with men who had fought in the Resistance. From early December the battalion had been attached to US 1st Army and tasked with guarding supply installations.

The platoon's officer, Lieutenant Detroz, flagged down Solis and told him that it was vital to prevent

Below: The fuel dump at Stavelot which was denied to Kampfgruppe Peiper *by the quick thinking of Major Paul Solis, the executive officer of 526th Armored Infantry battalion and Lieutenant Detroz of the 5th Fusilier Battalion of the Belgian Army.*

Right: A Republic P-47 Thunderbolt carrying bombs and rockets in a ground-attack role. The Thunderbolt entered service in 1943 as a long-range escort fighter but it was soon switched to the ground-attack role. Two attacks by P-47s seriously delayed Peiper's armoured column.

scavenging German units from capturing the fuel at Stavelot. As the ground on one side of the road rose sharply and dropped off equally sharply on the other, Solis and Detroz decided to build a barricade of jerrycans across the middle and set it ablaze. Although Peiper was unaware of the dump, a German patrol consisting of several tanks and halftracks was nosing towards it, probably to investigate the clouds of smoke billowing over the road. Confronted with a wall of flame that they could not bypass, the German armour turned back. A few hours later the fuel dump was secured by a battalion from the 30th Infantry Division.

This was not the last moment of frustration for *Kampfgruppe* Peiper. The delay in taking Stavelot allowed 1111th Engineer Combat Group to prepare a defence of the next town in Peiper's path, Trois Ponts, which was also the group's headquarters. At midnight on 17 December, C Company, 51st Engineer Combat Battalion, began preparing the town's bridges over the Amblève and Salm for demolition while a platoon of 291st Engineers tackled a bridge a mile to the south

Above: SS Lieutenant-Colonel Joachim Peiper, with the Death's Head emblem on his cap. His callous attitude to civilians and prisoners was the result of his Nazi beliefs and his experience on the pitiless Eastern Front, where his formation became known as the 'Blowtorch battalion'.

over the Salm. Luckily the engineers were reinforced by a 57mm (2.25in) antitank gun and crew of 526th Armored Infantry Battalion which had recently become separated from their unit.

By the time the leading tanks of *Kampfgruppe* Peiper moved out of Stavelot, the engineers had prepared the bridges for demolition. The lead vehicle of Peiper's column, a Panther, emerged from a railway underpass near the first bridge in Trois Ponts and was immediately engaged at close range by the crew of the antitank gun, who damaged one of the tank's tracks before being blown to pieces by the Panther's 75mm (2.95in) gun. Simultaneously, the two bridges in Trois Ponts were blown in a colossal blast of dust and debris, blocking Peiper's path into Trois Ponts, as the banks of the little river Amblève were too steep for his tanks. The bridge to the south of the town was blown minutes later as some of Peiper's paratroopers examined it for explosive charges.

Studying a map, Peiper saw that there was still another bridge over the Amblève at Cheneux, near the village of La Gleize. If he could seize this bridge, his column would be able to rejoin the road connecting Trois Ponts to Webermont and press on to the Meuse. Nevertheless, the loss of the bridge at

Trois Ponts was another bitter blow. Peiper would later observe that 'If we had captured the bridge at Trois Ponts intact, and had had enough fuel, it would have been a simple matter to drive through to the Meuse early that day.'

Kampfgruppe Peiper hurried on to La Gleize and found the bridge at Cheneux intact and able to bear the weight of its armour. However, shortly before crossing the bridge, Peiper's column, now stretching from La Gleize to Stavelot, was spotted by an American F-6 reconnaissance aircraft and came under attack from fighter-bombers of IX Tactical Air Command. Sixteen P-47 Thunderbolts bombed the column with 227kg (500lb) bombs and then made a succession of strafing runs. In a second attack, another 16 Thunderbolts attacked the head of Peiper's column while it was crossing the bridge at Cheneux, disabling several vehicles and losing one aircraft to ground fire. The exultant pilots subsequently made a wildly exaggerated claim of the damage they had inflicted, estimating that they had destroyed 32 armoured vehicles. What was of greater significance was the delay that the air attacks had imposed on *Kampfgruppe* Peiper. The attacks lasted about two hours, and after the fighter-bombers had flown away it took Peiper some time to get his column moving again. Moreover, 1st Army headquarters at Spa now knew exactly where Peiper was and where his column was heading.

Peiper was now making for Webermont but IX Tactical Air Command's attacks had bought precious time for men of A Company, 291st Combat Engineers, led by Lieutenant Alvin Edelstein, to wire the bridge at Habiémont and block the feeder roads with mines. It was growing dark when the combat engineers spotted the first German tank no more than 183m (200yd) away. It opened fire, and after an agonizing delay, the bridge was blown. Peiper pounded his knee with a fist, muttering through gritted teeth, 'The engineers! The damned engineers!'

Kampfgruppe Peiper withdrew northwards, and occupied La Gleize and the villages of Cheneux and Stoumont with the intention of turning them into a fortified triangle. By now, however, Peiper was coming under mounting pressure from 30th Infantry and 82nd Airborne Divisions. In his rear, Stavelot had been retaken by 30th Division, effectively blocking 1st SS Panzer Division's passage across the Amblève. Cut off from fuel and re-supply, the lifeblood of *Kampfgruppe* Peiper was draining away.

By 22 December, Peiper had been penned into La Gleize, which was under constant shellfire. The only chance of survival lay in a breakout to the east. On 21 December he had summoned his senior American prisoner, Major H.D. McCown of 30th Division, to his

command post. McCown, who knew of the massacre at Malmédy, was understandably apprehensive about the fate that might await the 150 American prisoners at the hands of the unnervingly amiable and cultured Peiper. Speaking in perfect English, Peiper gave McCown his word that the American men would be treated humanely, in accordance with the Geneva Convention.

The next day Peiper made a deal with McCown. He told the American that he wanted his assurances that the American commander who presently occupied La Gleize would return Peiper's wounded to German lines. In exchange for this, Peiper would leave behind all the American prisoners, with the exception of McCown, whom he would release once the German prisoners were repatriated. In response to this offer, McCown told him that he could do no more than sign a statement saying that he had heard the offer made by Peiper. To this, Joachim Peiper agreed, and the statement was written and signed before being given to another American officer, Captain Bruce Crissinger, to hold.

Above: Waffen-SS *troops riding in a SdKfz 251 halftrack in the Ardennes. Surrounded and out of fuel, Peiper's men were forced to abandon their vehicles and make a breakout from La Gleize to the east. Only 800 of Peiper's 5800 men who began the offensive were left.*

At around 13:00 hours the next day the remains of *Kampfgruppe* Peiper, now reduced to a rump of 800 men from the 5800 who had begun 'Autumn Mist', slipped out of La Gleize on foot. Crossing the River Amblève, they melted into the woods, hoping to pass through the lines of 82nd Airborne. Through the night, McCown trudged along beside Peiper. At daybreak Peiper indicated a fir tree bathed in brilliant sunlight, observing with heavy irony that it was the Christmas tree he had promised the American.

Near Trois Ponts, a firefight erupted, giving McCown the chance at last to escape and make his way back to American lines. However, Joachim Peiper evaded capture. He forded the river Salm and making contact with German forces some 6.5km (4 miles) to the east. They left behind them 353 prisoners and 111 civilians killed in cold blood.

CHAPTER SEVEN

Bastogne

To the German commander:

Nuts!

From the American commander.

General McAuliffe, 22 December 1944

The key to 5th Panzer Army's breakthrough was the road centre at Bastogne, and its capture was vital to the success of 'Autumn Mist'. Bastogne was a junction for the sparse network of highways that runs from the Eifel into the Ardennes and onward. A market town with a population of some 40,000, it stands on a plateau, the pastureland and rolling hills of which mark a vivid contrast with the broken, forested country which characterizes much of the Ardennes. The surrounding hills provide the town's only natural defence features, but the solidly built farmsteads that ring it in concentric circles offered anchors for defensive positions. Bastogne's main square, on the southern edge of the town, was the meeting point of five major and three secondary roads, making it of equal military importance to the Germans and Americans. For Hitler Bastogne was an exception to the rule he had demanded for 'Autumn Mist': that his Panzer formations bypass towns and leave the assault work to the infantry. He had given von Manteuffel permission to seize Bastogne with his panzers if he met stiff opposition there.

Eisenhower, too, grasped the importance of Bastogne. On the evening of 17 December he granted General Hodges' request for the movement of two

Left: Men of the 101st Airborne Division trapped in Bastogne on Christmas Eve singing hymns in a Christmas service. Although the men are not wearing their helmets, their rifles remain within arm's reach, ready for use should the Germans launch another attack.

airborne divisions, 82nd and 101st, to the general area of Bastogne to be committed under the command of XVIII Airborne Corps. At this early stage in the battle there was no intention of turning Bastogne into a fortress; rather the move was in recognition of the fact that the road network there would afford the Americans a number of options.

Bastogne was also demanding the attention of Major-General Troy H. Middleton, commander of VIII Corps. He was able to call on another division, 10th Armored, which had passed under his command with orders to counterattack the German thrusts north of Luxembourg City. Middleton now changed that order. The bulk of the division was to fulfil its original mission, but its leading combat command, then encamped near Luxembourg City, was to move with all possible speed on to Bastogne.

The commander of XVIII Corps, Major-General Matthew B. Ridgway, was in England conducting a postmortem on Operation 'Market Garden'. Acting as the corps commander was Major-General James M. Gavin, commander of 82nd Airborne and, at 37, the youngest divisional commander in the US Army. As 82nd Airborne had been out of the line longer than 101st following 'Market Garden', the division was to move first, at dawn on 18 December, to Bastogne. It was to be followed as soon as possible by 101st Airborne, which was to make for Webermont.

Dubbed the 'Screaming Eagles', after the savage bird on its shoulder patch, 101st Airborne had been badly mauled in Operation 'Market Garden', Montgomery's abortive attempt to bounce the Rhine, and had been resting, re-supplying and training replacements near Rheims, about 160km (100 miles) from the Ardennes. Its commander, Major-General Maxwell D. Taylor, was in Washington attending a conference, and the acting commander was Brigadier-General Anthony C. McAuliffe.

McAuliffe immediately put in hand preparations for the move to Webermont, the destination originally requested by General Hodges. Nearly 400 trucks were amassed, some of them from as far away as Paris, and the division's 11,000 men started moving out in combat teams at 09:00 hours on 18 December. It was a process that lasted all day and well into the night. McAuliffe and his G-2, Lieutenant-Colonel Harry W.O. Kinnard, went ahead in the former's command car. About 48km (30 miles) from Webermont they diverted to Middleton's VIII Corps headquarters, in Bastogne, at the Heintz barracks, in order to obtain a clear picture of the developing situation. The road leading from Bastogne was clogged with troops heading west, away from the front: an altogether unsettling phenomenon.

Below: The 101st Airborne march into Bastogne. Having been called into action with so little warning, many of the men lacked equipment, ammunition and even weapons. Some equipment was liberated from other retreating American troops to compensate.

McAuliffe was unaware that when General Gavin reached 1st Army headquarters in Spa, he had found Hodges increasingly alarmed by the threat of *Kampfgruppe* (Task Force) Peiper. As Gavin's division was ahead of McAuliffe's, Hodges ordered Gavin to move northwest to Webermont to block Peiper while 101st Airborne proceeded to Bastogne. Middleton's headquarters was to shift 32km (20 miles) to the southwest, to Neufchâteau. Gavin informed his convoy but the message did not reach McAuliffe. However, it reached Middleton and he passed the order on to McAuliffe. Darkness had not yet fallen when McAuliffe and Kinnard chose an assembly area to the west of Bastogne, at Mande-Saint-Etienne, and despatched a military policeman to a road junction to direct the march units of 101st's convoy to Bastogne. This was not a task that was easily accomplished, being hampered as it was by the many units withdrawing from Bastogne.

Around midnight on 18 December, the first units of 101st Airborne Division arrived in the assembly area near Bastogne. The men were sodden and frozen, having ridden in jolting trucks with no overhead cover. They had left their base near Rheims in such a hurry that many of the men did not have time to bring overcoats and overshoes, helmets and even weapons. They had little time to sleep or ready themselves for the battle that lay ahead. However, crucially, they had at last arrived at Bastogne.

Above: Watched by some of the locals, the 101st march through Bastogne to establish a defensive perimeter around the town. Bastogne was a vital objective for the Germans because many of the roads through the Ardennes met in the town.

At VIII Corps headquarters, Middleton had received another visitor, Colonel William L. Roberts, Commander of 10th Armored Division's Combat Command B. Roberts arrived at Middleton's headquarters in Bastogne at 16:00 hours. Middleton had already stared moving his headquarters troops to the rear, retaining only key staff members. He showed Roberts a map indicating that three German columns were bearing down on Bastogne along highways that converged in the town's main square. He asked Roberts how many combat teams he could muster.

Roberts replied that he could supply three combat teams. Middleton went on to say that once Roberts had made up the teams, he was to send one north of Bastogne to block the Liège highway at the village of Noville. The second was to be despatched to the southeast to block the highway leading from Ettelbruck. The third was to be sent to what seemed the point of greatest threat, the village of Longvilly.

Roberts listened warily. Middleton was an infantryman, inclined to parcel out armour in penny packets rather than concentrate it in strength to achieve deep penetrations in the manner approved by the Command and General Staff College, where Roberts had taught armoured doctrine. Roberts was thus reluctant to split his command but had to concede that Middleton, the corps commander, knew

more about the situation on the ground at Bastogne than he did. Middleton informed Roberts that he must hold these positions at all costs.

Roberts' three teams were deployed as follows. The first, commanded by Major William R. Desobry, consisted of about 400 men, including a company of Shermans, a company of armoured infantry, some engineers, medics and reconnaissance troops. Team Desobry was tasked with holding the village of Noville, a huddle of buildings on the Bastogne–Houffalize highway. The whole area was windswept and virtually treeless. The second team, commanded by Lieutenant-Colonel Henry T. Cherry (Team Cherry) comprised a medium tank company, two light tank platoons, an armoured infantry company and assorted medics, as well as engineers and reconnaissance troops. These men were to hold Longvilly, directly east of Bastogne. The third team, led by Lieutenant-Colonel James O'Hara (Team O'Hara) consisted of some 500 men and 30 tanks, and was to block the road from the southeast which ran into Bastogne from the nearby town of Wiltz.

The three teams took up their positions around Bastogne, passing on their way a constant flow of bedraggled, dispirited American troops trudging to the rear. When they reached Bastogne some kept on going, while others stayed. Colonel Roberts, who had experienced the retreat at Château-Thierry in May 1918, had sought and gained permission from Middleton to make use of stragglers. Those who stayed would play their part in the days ahead in a unit that would be dubbed Team SNAFU.

By the evening of 18 December, 101st Airborne had begun to assemble at Mande-Saint Etienne. McAuliffe decided to send the first unit to arrive, 501st Parachute Infantry Regiment, commanded by Colonel Julian J. Ewell, to reinforce Team Cherry along the road to Longvilly: 'Move out along this road to the east at 18:00, make contact with the enemy, attack and clear up the situation.'

Neither McAuliffe nor Ewell yet knew it, but the Parachute Infantry and Team Cherry were about to lock horns with one of Manteuffel's powerful armoured divisions, *Panzer Lehr*, commanded by Major-General Fritz Bayerlein, which had reached the village of Niederwampach, only 9.5km (6 miles)

Below: Brigadier-General Anthony McAuliffe, commander of the American troops besieged in Bastogne. A tough customer, McAuliffe had served in the artillery before transferring to the paratroops. For his defence of Bastogne, he was awarded the Distinguished Service Cross.

east of Bastogne. On the evening of 17 December, Manteuffel had been informed of an intercepted American radio message indicating that airborne troops would arrive in Bastogne either during the night of 18 December or early the next morning. The delays in 'Autumn Mist' were already threatening to dislocate the entire operation.

Bayerlein had already undermined his chances of seizing Bastogne in a *coup de main* by detaching a Panzergrenadier regiment and a special armoured breakthrough force to join attacks by von Luttwitz's XXXXVII Panzer Corps at Consthum and Hosingen. These units had suffered heavy casualties in both actions. Nevertheless, poised at Niederwampach on 18 December, Bayerlein could have brushed aside Team Cherry and driven all the way into Bastogne's main square before 501st Parachute Regiment could get underway. Instead, he took some poor advice.

Bayerlein was told by some Belgian civilians that an unpaved shortcut from Niederwampach led to the nearby settlement of Mageret which could be negotiated by his armour. In Mageret, Bayerlein could pick up the main road running to Bastogne. Bayerlein and a spearhead of 15 MkIVs plunged down the track, only to become enmired in a sea of mud. They took four hours to negotiate the short 5km (3 miles) to Mageret.

At Mageret, Bayerlein was once again given the run-around. Here he was told that a force of about 50 American tanks and an estimated 75 other vehicles, led by a major-general, had driven eastward through Mageret at midnight. In fact Bayerlein's eager informant had seen part of the less formidable Team Cherry. The report alarmed Bayerlein. He suspected that this phantom unit might prove too much for *Panzer Lehr*. At the very moment when it was imperative to drive forward, Bayerlein closed down for the night in Mageret, safe behind a minefield.

On the morning of 19 December, Bayerlein began to move westward towards Bastogne through heavy fog. As he entered the village of Neffe, one of his tanks hit a mine and was immediately disabled. Bayerlein stopped yet again. He was now on a collision course with Team Cherry and 1st Battalion, 501st Parachute Infantry Regiment, which was moving into Neffe, and ran into the advanced elements of *Panzer Lehr*. Rushing forward, the commander of 501st, Lieutenant-Colonel Ewell, told his men to stand their ground while he brought up the 2nd and 3rd Battalions. He despatched 2nd Battalion to the high ground around the neighbouring village of Bizory. When it arrived, the bulk of 3rd Battalion was positioned at Mont, on the Bastogne–Neffe road, with its southern flank protected by a company which was located in the village of Wardin.

Above: American troops march in front of an M3 halftrack. Introduced in 1941, the M3 was designed as a personnel carrier capable of moving an infantry squad. The vehicle also served as an artillery prime mover. In all, 54,000 US halftracks were built during World War II.

Below: German troops on a camouflaged halftrack with a flak gun mounted on its rear. The shortage of air cover forced the Germans to compensate with flak guns, but these were also used in a support role against ground targets.

Above: An American C-47, the mainstay of Allied air transport in all theatres, seen after a forced landing near Bastogne. The fog which was commonplace in the early part of the siege prevented an aerial resupply of the town, leading to ammunition and medical shortages.

At Wardin, the men of 1st Company arrived at the same time as a battalion of Panzergrenadiers supported by seven tanks. In the ensuing unequal fight, 1st Company stopped four of the German tanks but lost all its officers and 45 men, most of them killed or so gravely wounded that they had to be left behind. At Bizory, 2nd Battalion, tasked with taking Mageret, met 26th *Volksgrenadier*'s Reconnaissance Battalion and was stopped dead in its tracks.

Team Cherry had also been roughly handled in the clash with *Panzer Lehr*. A roadblock at Neffe held by Cherry's Reconnaissance Platoon was bulldozed aside and Cherry himself was bottled up in a château at the edge of the village where he had established his headquarters. He had to withdraw when it was set ablaze. Infiltrating German tanks created havoc as Cherry's forward units pulled back.

After trading heavy blows all day with *Panzer Lehr*, Ewell obtained permission from McAuliffe to establish a defensive line on high ground running south from Bizory, and was given a battalion of 327th Glider Infantry to strengthen his flank. Ewell's airborne troops and Team Cherry had prevented *Panzer Lehr* from breaking through to Bastogne.

An equally desperate battle had been raging at Noville, the village held by Major Desobry 9.5km (6 miles) northeast of Bastogne. The 26-year-old Desobry had been given some fatherly advice by Major-General Roberts on 18 December, before he had set off for Noville: 'By tomorrow morning, you'll probably be nervous. Then you'll probably want to pull out. When you begin thinking like that, remember I told you NOT to pull out.'

Desobry and his men arrived at the dreary settlement of Noville at about 23:00 hours. Desobry immediately set up a defence to the east, north and northwest, establishing outposts on the roads leading into the village. He gave instructions to his men to hang on to any stragglers who appeared willing to fight. From these stragglers, Desobry learned that a large German armoured force – 2nd Panzer Division – was fast approaching the village.

At about 04:00 hours the men Desobry had posted on the road leading from the east and the village of Bourcy heard halftracks approaching. A sentry, unsure whether they were American or German, yelled 'Halt!' Then, as the leading halftrack braked, someone shouted an order in German. The Americans opened fire from an embankment above the road, hurling grenades into the halftracks below them, before pulling back to Noville. The halftracks then retreated towards Bourcy.

Over an hour elapsed before the men holding Noville heard a rumbling noise in the distance which grew to a steady roar. German armour was moving past Noville along a road that bypassed the village to the north. At 06:00 hours the men in the outpost on

the road to Houffalize heard the rattle of approaching tanks. The men held their fire: the newcomers could be more American stragglers. They were MkIVs which knocked out the two Shermans at the outpost. Desobry ordered the survivors and the men holding the other two outposts to fall back.

By now daylight was beginning to penetrate the dense fog which blanketed Noville. Two more German tanks, followed by Panzergrenadiers, pushed down the road under a hail of American fire. The tanks blew up, partially blocking the road, and the Panzergrenadiers fell back down the Houffalize road. The fog lifted at about 10:30 hours to reveal on the high ground to the north at least 14 German tanks in a skirmish line; the ridgeline to the northeast was also swarming with armour. Team Desobry was facing an entire panzer division.

In the swirling fog that returned to Noville, lifted and then descended again, an armoured slugging match broke out. The open ground was a killing field for the Panzergrenadiers, so the fight for Noville was conducted at long range. Reinforced by a platoon

Above: A team of engineers returns from a night patrol on the Bastogne perimeter, heavily laden with bazookas. The fog and snow made it very difficult to distinguish landmarks, and it was easy for soldiers of both sides to lose their way and wander into enemy lines.

of self-propelled guns from 609th Tank Destroyer Battalion, Team Desobry hit 9 of the 14 tanks on the ridge, setting 3 on fire. Another tank heading into Noville along a farm track was hit and burst into flames; an armoured car scored a lucky hit on a Panther and knocked it out. In this battle, 2nd Panzer lost 17 tanks. Team Desobry's losses were 1 tank destroyer, 4 smaller vehicles and 13 wounded.

Despite the morning's successes, Desobry realized that his force was hopelessly outnumbered and was doomed to destruction in detail by German armour and artillery pouring fire down on Noville from the higher ground to the north and northeast. Desobry's thoughts turned to withdrawal and he radioed Major-General Roberts for permission to pull back 1.6km (1 mile) to higher ground and the village of Foy. He was told to use his own judgement and also

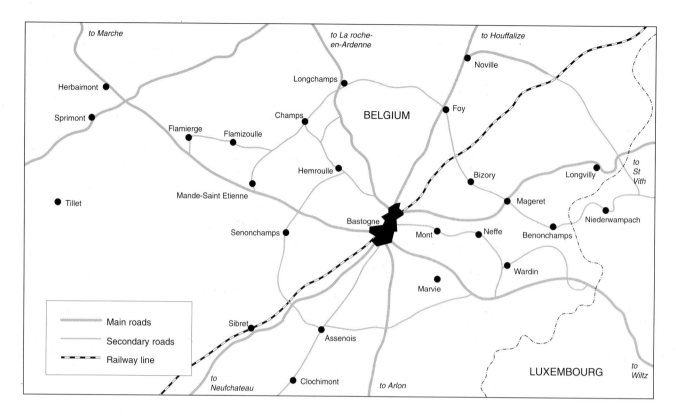

to Marche
to La roche-en-Ardenne
to Houffalize

Noville

Herbaimont

Longchamps

BELGIUM

Sprimont

Champs
Foy

Flamierge
Flamizoulle

to St Vith

Hemroulle
Bizory
Longvilly

Tillet
Mande-Saint Etienne
Mageret

Niederwampach

Bastogne
Mont
Neffe
Benonchamps

Senonchamps

Wardin

Marvie

Main roads

Secondary roads

Railway line

Sibret

Assenois

LUXEMBOURG
to Wiltz

to Neufchateau
Clochimont
to Arlon

Above: Bastogne and the villages around it. On a windswept plateau surrounded by wooded hills, and at the junction of several key roads, Bastogne was vital to 'Autumn Mist'. By holding it, the Americans halted the German build-up in the southern sector of the Ardennes.

Below: German troops outlined black against the snow. When the fog descended, the darkness of the uniforms concealed armour and men, but when it lifted, it left those who were without snow camouflage suits perilously exposed against a white background.

Above: The body of a German soldier lies frozen solid in a scene more reminiscent of Stalingrad than the western front. Although better equipped than their opponents in Bastogne, the Germans too suffered from the extreme cold at that time of year.

informed that a battalion of 506th Parachute Infantry, led by Lieutenant-Colonel James L LaPrade, was being rushed up from Bastogne to Noville. Desobry decided to hold on and to use the men of 506th to take the high ground from the Germans.

The attack went in during the early part of the afternoon, but nowhere did it gain more than 457m (500yd). The attack coincided with a German drive on Noville, which was halted at the edge of the village. Germans continued to bombard the village, and one 88mm (3.5in) shell killed LaPrade and wounded Desobry in the eye. He was rushed to 506th Parachute Infantry's aid station, then by ambulance to a collecting station west of Bastogne where surgeons saved his eye. Late that night the station came under German attack, and after a firefight the senior American officer there, Lieutenant-Colonel David Gould, surrendered. After avoiding capture earlier, Desobry was to become a prisoner of war.

In Noville, tanks and Panzergrenadiers continued to weave in and out of the murky fog in order to pick at the American defences. A Panther penetrated as far as a house that served as the command post for a company of armoured infantry. However, as the Panther swung its cannon towards the front door, it was driven off by a damaged Sherman tank.

By mid-morning on 20 December the fog lifted to reveal that the Germans had cut the road to Bastogne and had taken Foy. McAuliffe decided to

abandon Noville and at 13:00 hours the order was given to conduct a fighting withdrawal. This was a daunting prospect as the road to Foy ran ruler-straight from Noville through open fields affording no cover. The withdrawal went ahead, led by a company of paratroops on foot supported by three tanks. They were followed by four halftracks and five escorting trucks carrying the wounded. The rear of the column was brought up by a motley collection of vehicles protected by more paratroops on foot and four tank destroyers. As an ammunition dump was blown, the fog closed in again and the column moved off. It had crept to within 457km (500yd) of Foy, which was now back in American hands, when the leading halftrack ground to a halt and was rammed by the vehicle following it. Chaos followed as small-arms fire slashed into the head of the column and men all along it tumbled into the ditches. The column started moving again and, with machine guns on the leading halftracks blazing, soon gained the safety of Foy. After a delay, caused by the lead tank driver's reluctance to push into the fog, the column got underway again, but was halted by heavy German fire which disabled four tanks.

Above: Men of the US 4th Armored Division watch from their tank as C-47s fly in low over Bastogne after the skies had cleared sufficiently to allow operations to begin. The C-47s had been tasked with dropping in supplies for the defenders of the beleaguered town.

Below: One of the Allied airdrops over the surrounded town of Bastogne. Between 23 and 28 December, the C-47s dropped nearly 1000 tonnes of badly needed supplies at a cost of 19 aircraft shot down and 50 badly damaged.

The road was now blocked and the one functioning tank had been stranded as its driver had walked forward to try to start one of the halted tanks. Paratroopers called for volunteers to drive the tank but there were no takers from among the men of 10th Armored. In truth, they were for the most part replacements from other formations – cooks, mechanics and riflemen – and there were no drivers among them. However, this did not stop the paratroopers calling them 'yellow bastards'.

Beyond Foy, the column was still coming under fire from German armour, which was quickly driven off by one of the rearguard's tank destroyers. Freed from the German tanks' harassing fire, the remaining men and vehicles, including those bearing the wounded, worked their way off to the west of the road. By now the fifth tank had been got underway by the paratroopers and was lurching to safety.

Darkness was falling when the last of the survivors from the fight at Noville arrived in Bastogne. Team Desobry had lost 11 of its 15 medium tanks, 5 tank destroyers and about half its officers and men. Losses in 1st Battalion of 506th Parachute Infantry had been 212 killed, wounded and missing. Significantly, however, in the grim fight at Noville 2nd Panzer had lost some 30 tanks and up to 800 men. In the process, its drive to the Meuse had been delayed by at least 48 hours. Its commander was now ordered to forget about Bastogne and head for the Meuse. The task of taking Bastogne was to be left to *Panzer Lehr* and 26th *Volksgrenadier* Division.

By 20 December, Brigadier-General McAuliffe was edging ahead in the race to reinforce Bastogne. At his disposal was 101st Airborne and Combat Command B from 10th Armored. Another arrival was 705th Tank Destroyer Battalion from 9th Army equipped with long-barrelled self-propelled guns. McAuliffe deployed his forces in an arc around Bastogne, massing seven artillery battalions, including three long-range howitzer battalions, in the centre.

Throughout the day, the Germans continued to probe McAuliffe's perimeter, taking heavy punishment from his massed artillery. Late in the day, McAuliffe was driven in a jeep to Neufchâteau for a meeting with Middleton at which he assured the commander of VIII Corps that Bastogne could hold out, adding that if he withdrew now 'we'd be chewed to pieces'. Shortly after he returned to Bastogne, the Germans closed the ring around the town. That night Lieutenant-Colonel Kinnard told XVIII Airborne headquarters that the defenders of Bastogne were like 'a hole in a doughnut'.

The encirclement of Bastogne was followed by a two-day lull as the Germans massed for a fresh assault on McAuliffe's perimeter. The men of 101st Airborne remained calm; encirclement held no terrors for the airborne troops as they waited for a breakthrough force to relieve them. Kinnard took quiet satisfaction from his opinion that his men were now engaged in a 'textbook situation'.

Nevertheless, McAuliffe was worried about supplies. Ammunition for rifles and artillery was running low. All the gunners had dug pits that enabled them to fire their pieces in any direction but ate into the stocks of ammunition. By the evening of 21 December it was clear that shells would have to be conserved to deal with any crises, allowing German halftracks and tanks, bypassing Bastogne to the north and south, to move around with relative impunity while American infantry commanders and artillery forward observers ground their teeth in frustration. By noon on 22 December all four of 101st Airborne's artillery battalions were down to 200 shells each; McAuliffe was contemplating a daily ration of 10 rounds per gun.

Food and medical supplies were also in short supply. The medical unit attached to 101st Airborne had been taken prisoner on 19 December, and in Bastogne all the aid stations had become makeshift clinics. The wounded were piling up as no one could be evacuated. Seriously wounded men lay on the floor wrapped in blankets while exhausted surgeons moved about them. In a church located near the centre of Bastogne, patients of 501st Parachute Infantry's aid station lay in rows so tightly packed that surgeons had hardly any room to walk between them. Two surgeons worked without rest in an alcove in front of the altar. The overflow from the church were housed in a nearby garage, the men wrapped in blankets, on a layer of sawdust.

At midday on 22 December, at a farm near the Arlon highway, men from F Company, 327th Glider Infantry, watched in amazement as four Germans appeared in their foxhole line under a white flag. Two sergeants, Oswald Y. Butler and Carl E. Dickinson, left their command post in the farmhouse to investigate. They were accompanied by a medical aid man, Private First Class Ernest D. Permetz, who was chosen because he spoke German.

The Germans, two enlisted men and two officers from the operations section of *Panzer Lehr*, announced that they wanted to talk to the Americans' commanding general. The two American sergeants led the Germans to the farm where the enlisted men were left under guard. The officers were then blindfolded and led by Lieutenant Leslie E. Smith to the company command post. There they handed the company commander, Captain James F. Adams, a message typed in English and German. This was an ultimatum from 'The German

Commander' addressed to 'The USA Commander of the encircled town of Bastogne'. It stated that there was only one 'possibility' to save the encircled American troops from 'total annihilation' and that was honourable surrender. The American commander was to have two hours in which to consider the ultimatum. If it was rejected, the town of Bastogne would be flattened by German artillery and many civilians killed, an outcome inconsistent with the image of 'the well-known American humanity'.

The message was presented to McAuliffe's chief of staff, Lieutenant-Colonel Ned D. Moore, in the Heintz barracks by 327th Glider Infantry's operations officer, Major Alvin Jones. McAuliffe asked Moore what it said. Moore told him, 'They want us to surrender', to which McAuliffe retorted, 'Aw, nuts!' But how should he reply to the German ultimatum? Kinnard suggested that 'the first crack you made' would be appropriate. And thus it was that McAuliffe's written reply, one of the most celebrated of the war, was 'To the German commander: Nuts! From the American commander.'

When the two German officers were informed of McAuliffe's response, they were nonplussed, asking if it was negative or affirmative. They were left in no

doubt by Colonel Joseph H. Harper, commander of 327th Glider Infantry: 'The reply is decidedly not affirmative, and if you continue this foolish attack, your losses will be tremendous. If you don't understand what "Nuts!" means, in plain English it's the same as "Go to hell!"' The Germans were sent back on their way by Harper who – somewhat incongruously – wished the men good luck.

The surrender demand had been concocted by the commander of XXXXVII Panzer Corps, General Luttwitz. Manteuffel, who had not been consulted about it, was livid when he learned of it, not least because he lacked the artillery to make good Luttwitz's threat. To compensate for this, Manteuffel resolved to show the Americans the true nature of German might: he would bomb Bastogne.

On 23 December, the damp, foggy weather broke and bright, clear and cold weather greeted the defenders of Bastogne. For the first time since 16 December, Allied aircraft could enjoy conditions perfect for flying. By noon, the streets of Luxembourg City were packed with people craning their necks to watch the parade of air power overhead as 9th Air Force went on the offensive in the Ardennes sector. The sky seemed full of aircraft: B-26 medium bombers, P-47 and P-36 fighter-bombers, 'like shoals of silver minnows in the bright winter sun'.

At Bastogne the break in the weather heralded a desperately needed airdrop. At 09:00 hours teams of pathfinders parachuted in to mark the drop zone.

Below: Men of 101st Airborne drag much-needed medical supplies to safety at Bastogne. Very few supplies landed behind German lines. Allied air-lift capacity was essential to maintaining the troops who were tasked with defending the town.

Three hours later defenders of Bastogne heard the drone of approaching aircraft as gaggles of C-47 transports came into view, flying at an altitude of about 300m (1000ft). From their bellies dropped a stream of parachutes: red, yellow, orange blue and white. As soon as they flew in, German antiaircraft gunners opened up in response.

A total of 241 aircraft dropped 144 tonnes of supplies, only a few of which fell behind German lines. Over the next four days – excluding Christmas Day when the weather was poor over air bases in England – 962 C-47s dropped 850 tonnes of supplies. On 26 December there were also 11 gliders, some of which delivered surgeons. During the five days of air supply, the Germans shot down 19 planes and badly damaged another 50.

The C-47s' fighter-bomber escorts also attacked the German ring around Bastogne, where vehicle tracks in the snow indicated assembly areas in the surrounding forests, which were set ablaze in bomb and napalm attacks. In five days, these fighter-bombers flew an average of 250 sorties per day.

The clearing weather also enabled the commander of 9th Air Force, Major-General Hoyt S. Vandenberg, to activate a plan he had devised to attack the enemy's armoured spearheads, their supply chain in the Ardennes and the railheads and communications centres in the Eifel which were sustaining them. To maintain the pressure, two groups of P-51s were sent to Europe from bases in England. Now that Montgomery was temporarily in command of forces on the north side of the Ardennes 'bulge', British fighter-bombers also became available to operate in the Ardennes sector. As a result IX and XXIX Tactical Air Commands passed to the operational control of the British 2nd Tactical Air Force, although its commander, Air Marshal Sir Arthur Coningham, was careful to pay heed to the tactical input of IX Tactical Air Command and placed British

Below: Christmas Day in Bastogne. American morale soared after the defeat of the last serious German attempt to take the town, the arrival of para-dropped supplies in quantity, and the news that a relieving force was approaching the town.

Above: Hawker Typhoons of British 2nd Tactical Air Force which were tasked with aiding the American 9th Air Force in their efforts to disrupt the German offensive now that the weather had cleared up. The Typhoon, like the P-47, was a superb ground-attack aircraft.

units at its disposal to fly escorts and raid German airfields. These units were also tasked with the responsibility of flying armed reconnaissance along the Rhine, as well as providing close support for the ground troops.

On 23 December the cold weather had also come to the aid of the Germans. Their tanks could now race across the frozen ground. It fell to Colonel Heinz Kokott to press home the assault with 26th *Volksgrenadier* Division, reinforced with tanks and Panzergrenadiers of *Panzer Lehr*. Kokott planned to drive into Bastogne from the southeast and northwest, approaches he had correctly identified as being weakly defended. The southern perimeter was held by the glider troops commanded by Colonel

Joseph H. Harper, the officer who had wished good luck to the departing German surrender delegation. The 2.5km (1.5 miles) of front between the town of Marvie and the Arlon road was held by 300 men of 327th Glider Infantry, which came under heavy attack as darkness set in on 23 December. It seemed as if Colonel Kokott was about to prise open a chink in Bastogne's defences as *Panzer Lehr* gained a foothold in Marvie, only to be thrown back by the insertion of Team Cherry and a platoon of 501st Parachute Infantry to plug the gap.

On Christmas Eve at about 20:30 hours the bombers ordered up by Manteuffel arrived over Bastogne. The night was lit by the dazzling light of magnesium flares, then the bombs started falling. The first sticks fell close to the Heintz barracks. Fred MacKenzie, a war correspondent from the *Buffalo Evening News* and the only newsman in Bastogne, was sheltering in the basement of the barracks. He later wrote of 'an all but imperceptible movement sweeping along the passage' and of men 'drawing their physical parts into tight knots to resist shock' before a 'thunderous roar beat down on their senses'.

The bombers were principally Ju 88s, obsolete in a bombing role and an indication of the decayed state of the *Luftwaffe*, but they still inflicted heavy damage on Bastogne, reducing the area around the

Above: On Christmas Day the Germans launched their last serious attempt to take Bastogne, and some tanks penetrated as far as Hemroulle, about 1.6km (1 mile) from Bastogne. However this was to be the high-water mark of the German attempt to take the town.

main square to charred ruins. Earlier that night the defenders of Bastogne had received a Christmas message from McAuliffe: 'What's merry about all this? We're fighting – it's cold – we aren't home.' But, he went on, the troops 'were giving our country and our loved ones a worthy Christmas present'.

On Christmas Day, Colonel Kokott launched an all-out attack on Bastogne. He had intended to throw in the entire weight of 15th Panzergrenadier Division, which had served in Italy until the late summer of 1944. During the autumn it had been used as a fire brigade in the West, fighting at Aachen and in the Vosges. In the event, he was given an understrength Panzergrenadier regiment, two battalions of self-propelled artillery and 18 MkIV and Panther tanks. Kokott beefed up his reinforcement with one of his *Volksgrenadier* regiments and the greater part of his divisional artillery.

The *Volksgrenadiers* and Panzergrenadiers, wearing white snow camouflage and with their armour painted white, launched their attack at 03:00 hours on Christmas morning. They concentrated on two weak spots in the American perimeter: the sector held by 502nd Parachute Infantry at the village of Champs, 3km (2 miles) north of the Marche highway; and the sector occupied by Lieutenant-Colonel Jack G. Allen's battalion of 327th Glider Infantry between Champs and the highway.

Tanks and Panzergrenadiers broke through to Allen's command post, sending the Colonel and his staff racing to the rear as the tanks lumbered through the lifting murk, Panzergrenadiers clinging to their hulls. The tanks pressed on towards the command post of 502nd Parachute Infantry which was located in the Château Rolle, half a mile behind Champs. German armour was also bearing down on two companies of 502nd Parachute Infantry which were marching to the relief of Champs. The paratroopers retreated to the cover of woodland; with harassing fire, they forced the Panzergrenadiers to abandon their mounts and seek cover.

In a fierce exchange of fire, self-propelled guns of 705th Tank Destroyer Battalion knocked out three of the tanks, and paratroopers accounted for another with a bazooka. Another tank ploughed on towards Champs but was knocked out by the paratroopers

there. A seventh tank turned back towards Hemroulle, where it surrendered after coming under heavy fire. For one tantalizing moment, Kokott believed that his armour had penetrated to Bastogne, but the tank commander who had radioed success had confused Hemroulle with Bastogne, which lay about 1.6km (1 mile) away. Eleven German tanks had burst into the village where they were halted and knocked out by intense fire from American tanks, tank destroyers, parachute field artillery battalions and bazookas. Kokott was to launch another attack before daylight on the morning of 26 December but this was little more than the twitching of a corpse. The chance of seizing Bastogne had passed him by.

For several days, Kokott had been looking over his shoulder for an American army driving up from the south to relieve Bastogne. Now it had arrived. For four days, 4th Armored Division had been fighting its way northward in order to lift the siege. On the afternoon of 26 December, its lead elements were only 6.5km (4 miles) south of Bastogne. They were 37th Tank Battalion, commanded by Lieutenant-Colonel Creighton W. Abrams, and 53rd Armored Infantry Battalion, which was commanded by Lieutenant-Colonel George L. Jacques. Along with an armoured artillery battalion and a battery of 155mm (6.1in) howitzers, these units combined together to make up Combat Command R.

Below: General Maxwell Taylor (right), commander of the 101st Division, shakes hands with Brigadier-General Anthony McAuliffe after the relief of Bastogne. Taylor had been on leave when the battle began, and was forced to watch the siege from the sidelines.

On 26 December, Abrams and Jacques were standing at a road junction, discussing their next move. They had planned an attack on the village of Sibret, which Abrams knew was held by strong German forces. He was concerned that an assault on the village might expose his own flank to a counter-attack. However, the two officers' deliberations were interrupted by the passage overhead of an air armada, comprising C-47s on their way to re-supply Bastogne. Sucking on a big cigar, Abrams turned to Jacques and proposed that they forget about Sibret and roar straight through to Bastogne by way of a secondary road which ran from the village of Assenois. They decided that they would not inform their commander, Colonel Wendell Blanchard, of their intentions to take this direct route.

Dusk was setting in when six of Abrams' Shermans, commanded by First Lieutenant Charles P. Boggess, moved ahead. These Shermans were followed by armoured infantry who were riding in their halftracks. As he neared Assenois, Boggess radioed to ask for artillery fire. Abrams himself called it up, putting in a request for 'Concentration Number Nine: play it soft and sweet'.

Four artillery battalions and a battery of 155s sent 420 rounds into Assenois and the woods that flanked the road. The artillery was still dropping shells into the centre of the village when Boggess and his tanks finally moved in, followed by the halftracks, and as a result one of the halftracks was hit by friendly fire. The armoured infantrymen jumped down and began to sweep the town. Simultaneously, a large body of Germans – which was made up of paratroops and *Volksgrenadiers* – emerged from the cellars in which the men had been sheltering. A close-quarters fight for Assenois then began in earnest.

Above: Men of the 4th Armored Divison, who were responsible for the lifting of the siege of Bastogne, on the march towards the beleaguered town on 27 December 1944. In the distance is a plume of smoke from an artillery shellburst.

Boggess, followed by four tanks and a stray half-track that had been sucked into the column, pressed on to the woods behind the town where the trees overhung the road; his machine guns sprayed the undergrowth on either side. The halftrack hit a mine and the tanks following it fell behind. While one of them pinned down the Germans in the woods, the survivors from the halftrack set about clearing more mines from the road. Their work done, they jumped aboard the Shermans and raced to catch Boggess, who had now cleared the wood and was fast approaching an old Belgian pillbox. Nearby, some American infantry seemed to be preparing to attack it. Boggess' gun dealt with the pillbox in short order, sending the mystery American troops scrambling for cover. Standing in his open turret, Boggess yelled, 'Come here! This is 4th Armored!'

As the men emerged, their commander, Lieutenant Duane J. Webster of 326th Airborne Engineer Battalion, came forward to shake Boggess by the hand and asked him if he had any water: his men had had only melted snow to drink that day. Together the Americans drank a toast.

At one of 326th Airborne's observation posts was General McAuliffe, who had hurried forward when he had received the news that contact had been made with friendly tanks. There he warmly greeted Boggess' commanding officer, Captain William Dwight. 'Gee', exclaimed a jubilant McAuliffe, 'I am mighty glad to see you.' At last, the siege of Bastogne had come to an end.

CHAPTER EIGHT

The Tables Turned

Undoubtedly the greatest American battle of the War,
[the Battle of the Bulge] will, I believe, be regarded
an ever-famous American victory.

Prime Minister Winston S. Churchill, 18 January 1945

The relief of Bastogne had come at a price. The men of 4th Armored Division had been ordered by Patton to 'drive like hell', just as they had across France in the summer of 1944, but they had encountered determined German opposition, principally from 5th Parachute Division, and atrocious weather conditions that ranged from snowstorms to seas of mud. When the temperature plummeted, the roads resembled ice rinks. These problems were compounded by the fact that the division was short of tanks, and many of those in service were worn and prone to breakdowns. For its newly appointed commander, Major-General Hugh J. Gaffey, the Ardennes was to be a baptism of fire with a divisional command. There were also many replacements among the tank crews and armoured infantry.

Nevertheless, when 4th Armored began its northward thrust on 22 December, optimism ran high that it would slice its way through to Bastogne in two days to open up a supply corridor to the besieged town. At first it seemed likely that these confident hopes would be realized. On 22 December, good progress was made by the division's two spearhead units, Combat Command A (CCA) and Combat Command B (CCB). Combat Command A advanced

Left: 'All this fresh air is going to be the death of me.' The final phase of the Battle of the Bulge was accompanied by savage weather conditions. The GIs' rifles sometimes froze and could only be unjammed in action by the soldiers urinating on them. Frostbite was endemic.

13km (8 miles) to Martelange, while Combat Command B drove 19km (12 miles) to Burnon. Both units were then halted by bridges that had recently been blown by the Germans.

On 23 December, as Bastogne received its first big air drop, Combat Command A was bogged down in German-held Martelange while engineers threw a 30m (90ft) Bailey bridge across the gorge of the River Sure. Once across, hard fighting awaited CCA at Warnach. Its German defenders inflicted heavy casualties during a succession of assaults.

Meanwhile, CCB crossed the Sure at Burnon, 11km (7 miles) from Bastogne, and then took Chaumont, only to experience a terrible pounding from five Ferdinand tank destroyers – long-barrelled 88mm (3.47in) guns on a Tiger chassis – which had arrived from Italy and were part of 653 Heavy *Panzerjäger* Battalion. The Americans were forced to withdraw. More encouraging progress was made by the division's reserve, Combat Command R (CCR) which, advancing parallel to CCA to protect the right flank, took Bigonville. That night, McAuliffe sent a message to 4th Armored Division: 'Sorry I did not get to shake hands today. I was disappointed.' This was followed by a note from an officer on his staff: 'There is only one more shopping day before Christmas!'

On Christmas Eve, CCA fought all day to push past Warnach while CCB strove to retake Chaumont, only to be thrown back. On the right of the advance, CCR had a hard fight for Bigonville in which the town's defenders fought on until they had all but exhausted their ammunition.

At dawn on Christmas Day, as the defenders of Bastogne clung on to the town's buckling perimeter, a few kilometres to the southwest, 4th Armored's combat commands were still held up by German roadblocks and antitank crews, concealed along the edges of dense woodland, who raked American armour and infantry as they crossed open ground. By now, however, Lieutenant-Colonel Abrams was contemplating the dash through Assenois that would link 4th Armored with the defenders of Bastogne. The northward drive by 4th Armored had been achieved at a cost of 1400 casualties.

On 23 December, while 4th Armored Division was battling towards Bastogne, Major-General Ernest N. Harmon, commander of US 2nd Armored Division, lunched with his staff at their new command post, a château in the village of Havelange, 32km (20 miles) east of the Meuse. The 'Hell on Wheels' division had arrived in the Ardennes on 22 December, after a 113-km (70-mile) forced march from the Aachen sector.

Below: American Sherman tanks from 4th Armored covering the countryside near Bastogne as they await the order to advance during Patton's push into the German salient from the south. The division had seen fierce fighting on its way to lift the siege of Bastogne.

Harmon, who was famous for his bass tones – he was dubbed 'Old Gravel Voice' – had originally commanded 2nd Armored in North Africa and had rejoined it in Normandy. Earlier that day he had paid a visit to his Corps Commander, Major-General Lawton J. 'Lightning Joe' Collins, at his VII Corps command post in the Château de Bessines, 16km (10 miles) north of Marche. Collins had told him that he hoped to keep the arrival of 2nd Armored concealed from the Germans long enough for it to be used in a surprise attack. He should not expect to go into action for at least a week, perhaps 10 days.

Towards the end of lunch, a young officer with a bandaged head, Lieutenant Everett C. Jones, interrupted the coffee with the news that at a village 16km (10 miles) to the south near the town of Ciney, his patrol from 82nd Armored Reconnaissance Battalion had come under fire from a number of German armoured vehicles, including two MkIVs.

It later emerged that the tanks were in fact a British patrol probing east of Dinant, but this announcement electrified Harmon. Clearly his division's presence had been revealed to the enemy and a German armoured spearhead was heading towards the Meuse. Racing across a field to a copse where one of his tank battalions was laagered, Harmon asked a company commander how long it would

Above: American troops clamber aboard an abandoned Panther which had been left behind after a shell had jammed in the breech of its 75mm (2.95in) gun. The failure of 'Autumn Mist' cost the Germans heavily in terms of lost men and matériel that were irreplaceable.

take to get his vehicles on the road. Five minutes, replied the commander, as long as radio silence was lifted. Harmon told him that silence was lifted from that moment. 'You get down that road to a town called Ciney … block the exits and entrances and start fighting. The whole damn division is coming right behind you!'

To the east of 2nd Armored lay 2nd Panzer Division, the spearhead of the German drive to the Meuse. Its commander, Colonel Meinrad von Lauchert, had raced ahead by avoiding the entanglements that had dogged the armoured formations on which Hitler's hopes had rested. Lauchert had pushed through the gap between St Vith and Bastogne, passed northeast of Bastogne, where he was detained by a day of fierce fighting, and continued westward when it became clear that the town would not fall without a bitter struggle. On 23 December, 2nd Panzer swept south of the American-held town of Marche. As dusk drew in, its leading elements were 24km (15 miles) from the Meuse.

There was a price to pay for this success. By 23 December, 2nd Panzer was advancing alone, having outstripped 116th Panzer Division to the north and

Panzer Lehr to the south, and was thus increasingly vulnerable to flank attack by the Americans. It was strung out in a 19km (12-mile) column, its men exhausted and its armour running low on fuel.

Von Manteuffel was torn between his desire to reach the Meuse and his concern about the increasingly exposed position of 2nd Panzer. He had ordered *Panzer Lehr* to join 2nd Panzer in the final push for the Meuse, but it was not until 22 December that the main body of *Panzer Lehr*, which had left behind a panzergrenadier regiment at Bastogne, began moving towards the Meuse. Lack of fuel caused further delays and by noon on 23 December, with Manteuffel personally urging them on, *Panzer Lehr* moved into the Rochefort area, 24km (15 miles) from the Meuse. Rochefort was taken after a sharp fight with a battalion of 335th Infantry, and there Bayerlein called a halt, as his men were utterly exhausted.

Above: British Shermans similar to those stumbled upon by 2nd Panzer Division during their push towards the Meuse at Dinant. The British tankers were literally caught napping, but a lucky hit on a German ammunition truck saw the Germans retreat back to a nearby village.

On the night of 23 December, Manteuffel conferred with von Luttwitz, commander of XXXXVII Panzer Corps. Manteuffel noted that the Americans held the town of Marche, 32km (20 miles) due west of Dinant, in strength, thus blocking the path to Namur. However, 2nd Panzer Division had bypassed Marche to the south and *Panzer Lehr* was poised to push west beyond Rochefort into the valley of the River Lesse. From Rochefort to the Meuse at Dinant was only 23km (14 miles).

However, Manteuffel was aware of the peril inherent in the present situation. The two panzer divisions were little more than a 'pointed wedge' with two open flanks, which would have to be protected by dropping off troops as they pushed forward. Much depended on the imminent arrival of 9th Panzer Division to protect 2nd Panzer's north flank at Marche. Manteuffel also intended to make a personal call on General von Waldenburg, the commander of 116th Panzer Division, to encourage him to cut the Marche–Hotton highway as well as Highway N-4 behind it. This would prevent

American reinforcements coming through Marche to take the Germans in the north flank. Thereafter Waldenburg was to push on to Ciney, extending the protection he was affording Manteuffel's northern flank. Manteuffel did not consider this an ideal solution, but it was the one most likely to get him to the Meuse. However, he was still unaware that he was about to encounter the weight of Harmon's 2nd Armored Division, part of which had already engaged advanced elements of 2nd Panzer.

The Germans had run into units of a task force led by Lieutenant-Colonel Hugh O'Farrell, commander of 66th Regiment's 2nd Battalion. Near the village of Haid, F Company of 41st Armored Infantry collided with a German column headed by troops who were riding in American jeeps and trucks. All hell broke loose, and in the firefight the Germans were overwhelmed. A total of 30 Germans were killed and the same number marched to the rear as prisoners.

Later that morning, at about 06:00 hours, advanced elements of 2nd Panzer were pushing through a bank of fog towards Celles, 6.5km (4 miles) from the Meuse. Here the column was delayed when a Panther hit a mine. The tanks were now critically low on fuel and a crew enquired of a local hotelier, Madame Marthe Monrique, how far it was to Dinant. Though she gave them a truthful

Above: The Ardennes winter was as tough an enemy as the Germans. Bradley admitted that there was insufficient winter gear: 'I had deliberately bypassed shipments of winter clothing in favour of ammunition and gasoline. We had gambled on our choice and now we were paying.'

Below: As Allied success grew and the failure of Hitler's gamble became obvious, increasing numbers of prisoners were taken by the advancing troops of Patton's 3rd Army. However, Hitler ordered his troops to fight hard to hold on to the territory they had won at such cost.

Left: German infantry trudge forward to their positions carrying boxes of machine gun ammunition. Each box could carry a belt of 250 rounds, and the handles were offset to the side to allow two to be easily carried in one hand.

sound asleep, and 2nd Panzer's reconnaissance formation probed forward, waking the slumbering British tankmen. A snap shot by Sergeant F. 'Geordie' Probert plunged into the German column, blowing up an ammunition truck and setting fire to the fuel-laden vehicle behind it. Dismayed by the unexpected resistance, and running low on fuel, the Germans withdrew to the nearby village of Foy-Notre Dame. There they stayed, 5km (3 miles) from the Meuse.

On the face of it, the situation at the eastern end of the Bulge driven into Ardennes by Manteuffel seemed to justify the ultra-cautious approach adopted by Montgomery as he busied himself with the tidying up of the Allied Front before the unleashing of a counterblow. Five panzer divisions were now at large, and a sixth was on the way: *Panzer Lehr* and 2nd Panzer Division were pushing past Marche to the Meuse; 116th Panzer was attempting to get on to the Condroz plateau to add weight to the drive; 2nd SS and 9th SS Panzer, on the other side of the River Ourthe, were also trying to get on to the plateau; and 9th Panzer was on the way to Marche. To Montgomery, this was evidence that another big punch was on the way, perhaps the heaviest blow to be landed throughout 'Autumn Mist'.

But appearances were deceptive. With the exception of 9th Panzer, all German armoured formations had been severely handled. Allied aircraft were now limiting German movement by day, and the fuel supplies and troops were approaching exhaustion. Nevertheless, the Meuse was a stone's throw away.

In the afternoon of 24 December, Major-General Harmon telephoned VII Corps in a state of high excitement. One of his patrols had spotted German armour around Celles, and Belgian civilians had informed it that the tanks had run out of fuel. Harmon was desperate to go on to the attack, but at VII Corps headquarters, where Major-General Collins was temporarily absent, there was understandable reluctance to override Montgomery's reshaping of the battlefield. After much deliberation, Collins gave permission for Harmon to go on to the offensive.

At 08:00 hours on Christmas morning, 2nd Armored Division launched an all-out assault against German armour at the tip of the Bulge. Combat

answer to this – 10km (6 miles) – she then ventured a pack of lies. During the night, Madame Monrique claimed, the Americans had laid mines along the road for miles, an assertion that had been lent credence by the loss of the Panther. After some delay, the column got underway again.

There were no Americans, but trouble waited in the form of five British-manned Shermans of 3rd Royal Tank Regiment which were guarding the west bank of the Meuse at Dinant. Their crews were

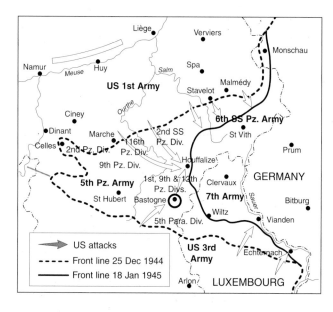

Left: The German salient was gradually squeezed by the American 3rd Army in the south and the American 1st Army in the north with the assistance of elements of the British XXX Corps. Progress was hindered by the poor weather conditions and dogged German defence.

Command B, led by Brigadier-General I.D. White, drove southwest to Celles in order to encircle and destroy the German armour there. Combat Command A headed southeast to Rochefort to block any new German drive to the Meuse.

During three days of fighting in and around the Celles pocket, 2nd and 9th Panzer and *Panzer Lehr* lost 82 tanks, 83 field guns and 441 vehicles. They sustained some 2500 casualties and 1200 men were taken prisoner. *Panzer Lehr* made two attempts to rescue 2nd Panzer from the pocket. On both occasions it was halted by British Typhoons and American P-38 fighter-bombers, the Typhoons being guided to their targets by 2nd Armored's spotter aircraft. To the north, 116th Panzer struggled towards Marche and was forced to dig in well short of the Meuse. It was now utterly finished as an offensive threat in the battle.

Some 64km (40 miles) to the east of Celles yet another German threat appeared at the remote crossroads of Baraque de Fraiture, from which a major north–south route, the N-15, ran to Liège. Alternatively, another of the roads branching from Baraque de Fraiture could feed reinforcements to Manteuffel's formations striving to reach the Meuse.

Above: American officers pose in front of an abandoned MkV Panther, its rear turret hatch gaping open. Fuel was in such short supply for the Germans that many serviceable vehicles were left behind for the Allies to capture solely because their tanks were empty.

Tasked with securing the road junction was 2nd SS Panzer Division, which had peeled away from Manteuffel's western thrust and driven north to the Baraque crossroads, which crowned a windswept 700m (2300ft) plateau and lay along the vulnerable boundary between 82nd Airborne and 3rd Armored divisions. These two formations were already badly stretched and, despite its obvious importance, the crossroads was untenanted. That was, until it was occupied by the enterprising Major Arthur C. Parker III, the executive officer of 589th Field Artillery Battalion, 106th Division, which had been virtually wiped out in the fighting on the Schnee Eifel.

On 19 December, Parker secured the crossroads with his three artillery pieces and their crews, plus a few men of 589th Battalion's Field Artillery Service Battery, also survivors of the Schnee Eifel: a total of 110 men. He was joined the next day by a detachment from an antiaircraft battalion with three half-tracks which mounted quad-50s and a self-propelled

37mm (1.46in) gun. At midday he chose to ignore an order to move his artillery pieces well to the rear where 589th Battalion was to be reconstituted.

Parker's improvised force withstood a succession of probing attacks from reconnaissance patrols which had been launched by 2nd SS Panzer Division, which was moving north from Houffalize to Baraque de Fraiture after failing to open the Salmchateau–La Roche highway. Late on 21 December, Parker was badly wounded by a fragment from a mortar shell and he was evacuated. Command then passed to Major Elliott Goldstein.

On the night of 22 December, Goldstein received further reinforcements: a troop of 87th Armored Reconnaissance Squadron and two self-propelled guns of 3rd Armored's Task Force Kane. Goldstein anticipated that his small force would soon take the full brunt of 2nd SS Panzer. The commander of 82nd Airborne, Major-General James Gavin, was increasingly concerned about the threat to N-15. If the Germans drove up the highway, they could either

trap 82nd Airborne in the angle which was formed by the Amblève and Salm rivers, or to force the division's withdrawal and compromise Gavin's mission of covering the exodus of troops from St Vith.

After consulting with the commander of 3rd Armored Division, Major-General Maurice Rose, Gavin sent a company of glider troops from his reserve 325th Battalion to the crossroads, and moved the rest of the battalion up to the high ground which overlooked the road junction. The troops were forced to move into position during a heavy snowstorm on 22 December.

These men were just in time to meet 2nd SS Panzer, which launched its attack in earnest on 23 December. After a 20-minute bombardment of American positions around the crossroads, a Panzergrenadier regiment attacked behind two companies of tanks. The defenders of Barraque held out for an hour before they were overwhelmed. Their gallant resistance had, nevertheless, bought vital time for Gavin, who had been handed orders found on a captured German regimental adjutant indicating that 2nd SS Panzer was launching a major drive to Manhay, threatening Gavin's weak right flank.

The swarms of Allied fighter-bombers now filling the skies by day did not encourage movement along

Below: Panthers of 2nd SS Panzer Division Das Reich *seen before the launch of their attack on Manhay. The thick forest gave the tanks cover from the attentions of the prowling Allied fighter-bombers, whose 127mm (5in) rockets could rip open their armour with ease.*

a narrow, forest-lined road. The commander of 2nd SS Panzer, Lieutenant-General Heinz Lammerding, planned to move through the villages on either side of the highway before converging on Manhay at a point where the woods thinned. In order to prepare the way, SS Panzergrenadiers infiltrated the woods on the night of 23 December, routing a platoon of light tanks and a squad of infantry between Manhay and Barraque. However, until the track through the woods could be improved, this success could not be exploited in order to enable the tanks to get through. This was a task which took longer than expected; it would not be completed until the early evening of 24 December, Christmas Eve.

Meanwhile, Gavin was still trying to shore up his right flank. Early on Christmas Eve morning, General Ridgway warned Gavin to prepare for a possible withdrawal. This was worrying news for Gavin. He was proud of the fact that his division had never yielded any ground it had taken. The spectacle of the exhausted and demoralized American troops streaming back from St Vith had made a lasting impression on him and his men. For his own men to withdraw so soon after this depressing experience was a prospect Gavin was reluctant to contemplate. Rumours sparked by the 'Greif' commandos operating in American uniform behind Allied lines were still flying around. Gavin had little wish to spark a general collapse of morale.

Below: A superb view of a Republic P-47 Thunderbolt. In addition to rockets and bombs, the Thunderbolt was armed with eight 12.7mm (0.5in) machine guns. From 23 December 1944, the Thunderbolts of 9th Air Force flew over 1000 ground attack sorties.

Above: Sepp Dietrich, commander of 6th SS Panzer Army, seen during a medal ceremony. Despite his scepticism, he carried out Hitler's orders to maintain the offensive and oversaw the continued German attempts to break through towards Antwerp.

On the morning of 24 December, Field Marshal Montgomery paid a visit to Ridgway's headquarters at Webermont. Monty arrived in an open car, jauntily acknowledged the sentries' salutes and hurried inside. He came straight to the point, telling Ridgway that 1st Army must build a solid northern flank by shortening the line in readiness for a counterattack by Collins' VII Corps. The new line was to run south-west from the solid positions established on the Eisenborn Ridge and at Malmédy and Stavelot. Studying the map, Montgomery and Ridgway agreed that the line was to extend from Trois Ponts along the road to Manhay, a line that Gavin had already reconnoitred. At Manhay – now the headquarters of 7th Armored's CCA – there was to be a sole outpost placed on high ground located behind the town. To the west of Manhay, 3rd Armored was to defend along the road which ran from Trois Ponts through Manhay to Hotton.

The reshuffling of the line did not get underway until darkness had fallen on the night of 24 December. It coincided with a renewed attack by 2nd SS Panzer towards the N-15 and Manhay, which fell on understrength units of 3rd and 7th Armored Divisions. In the confusion, the Germans gained the advantage and were able to take Manhay.

One of the most remarkable passages of arms in this battle occurred when 4th Company 1st Panzer Battalion drove on Manhay. In one of its Panthers was SS Sergeant Ernst Barkmann. As the German tanks manoeuvred into position, they were hit by a heavy American artillery bombardment that knocked out the leading vehicles. The ferocity of the artillery fire stopped the German armour in its tracks, but Barkmann roared ahead. His first victim was a Sherman, which he mistook in the dark for one of his own company's vehicles. By the time he realized his mistake, he was on top of the Sherman and had to reverse the Panther before he could open fire.

Barkmann forged on, knocking out two more tanks he encountered on the road. Rounding a bend, he saw a line of nine Shermans drawn up in a field. Approaching at a steady speed, so as not to arouse

suspicion, he adroitly manoeuvred his Panther into position from which only one of the Shermans could return fire. Before Barkmann could attack, the American crews abandoned their machines and fled. Rather than waste ammunition on the deserted tanks, he left them to be destroyed by his comrades following behind him and pressed on.

Barkmann then swung his Panther on to the main road to Manhay and sped past columns of retreating American infantry, none of whom identified his tank as hostile. However, his luck did not hold as he soon ran into a mass of vehicles of 2nd Armored Division, who clearly recognized the intruder. Barkmann ordered smoke to be laid and attempted to escape behind the screen. As the Panther ground forward, a jeep charged him, its driver signalling that he should halt. Ignoring this surreal intervention, Barkmann slammed into the jeep and then slid into a Sherman. Both tanks were temporarily locked together, and at this point Barkmann's engine chose to cut out. After several anxious moments it roared back into life, enabling Barkmann to disengage and race up the road pursued by another Sherman which Barkmann was able to knock out. In Manhay, Barkmann found

Above: Infantry of 2nd SS Panzer Division Das Reich *walk past blazing US vehicles near Manhay, on the northern shoulder of the Bulge, on 24 December. The SS division took the town that evening, briefly rekindling Hitler's dwindling hopes of reaching the Meuse.*

30 abandoned Shermans, but realizing that his remarkable fortune must eventually run out, he turned into the woods and drove on until he had regained contact with his battalion.

Early on Christmas morning, 2nd SS Panzer threw a few desultory stabs up the N-15 from Manhay. But by now General Lammerding's goal was not Liège, and after taking heavy fire, 2nd SS Panzer turned back, moving northwest to cross the River Ourthe and gain the Condroz plateau to protect the flank of 5th Panzer Army. For Lammerding, Manhay was not the jumping-off point for Liège, rather it was a pivot for his northwest turn. Unaware of this, Ridgway was determined to retake Manhay, and the battered 7th Armored was given the task, reinforced by 517th Parachute Infantry Regiment. Manhay passed back into American hands on 27 December, but by then it no longer figured in German plans. At Celles in the west, and Manhay in the north, 'Autumn Mist' had

163

reached its high-water mark. Adolf Hitler's great gamble had failed. Not a single German tank had crossed the Meuse.

Moving westward, 2nd SS Panzer took the town of Grandmenil, 1.6km (1 mile) from Manhay, only to be subsequently driven out by the counterattacking 3rd Armored Division. The battle had now conformed to Montgomery's cautious instincts. The German offensive had spent itself and was contained by the 19 British and American divisions gathered in and around the Ardennes salient. The mists that had masked the German concentration and initial assault had dispersed, and Allied aircraft were busily ranging all over the battlefield.

On Christmas Day, a Spitfire pilot, Flight Lieutenant Jack Boyle, of 411th Squadron based at Heesch airfield, had an encounter with a German Me 262 jet. Boyle's entire Wing, which consisted of five squadrons, including 411th, had been ordered to

Below: An Me 262, the first jet fighter to go into service anywhere in the world. Although they were potential war-winners, the Germans lacked sufficient machines and pilots to make a substantial difference to the air war.

provide maximum support in the sector around Bastogne. Boyle had been forced to turn back from his mission in order to escort a fighter which had been struck with engine trouble:

'I was sorely troubled by this turn of events and grumbled to myself all the way home about bad luck and fickle fate. As we neared the home base at Heesch, we were far too high and in an irritable mood. To get rid of the excess height I stuck the nose almost straight down in a screaming spiral dive. As my speed shot past 500mph [805km/h], out of nowhere appeared a German Me 262 jet. It only took a second to see to my gun-sight and safety catch and then I was right behind him. My first bursts of cannon fire hit his port engine pod and it began streaming dense smoke. He immediately dived for the deck as an evasive tactic, but with only one engine he couldn't outrun me. I scored several more hits before he clipped some tree tops and then hit the ground at an almost flat angle. His aircraft disintegrated in stages from nose to tail as it ripped the turf for several hundred yards until only the tailplane assembly was left and it went cartwheeling along just below me at about my speed. Fire and smoke

marked his trail. As I circled, farmers emerged from their barns and waved up at me.'

The battle in the Ardennes was taking on a new shape. In the American camp, relief that the crisis had passed was replaced by a bullish attitude. Bradley, convinced that the German drive had spent itself, urged an immediate counterattack. Predictably, Montgomery was more circumspect. US 1st Army, on the northern side of the Bulge, was still under his command and, in his opinion, it needed time to recover from the losses it had suffered before being turned on to the counteroffensive. In addition, there was still large amounts work to be done in order to secure the lifeline to Bastogne.

In the German camp there was also a reassessment. On 22 December, von Rundstedt had urged Hitler to call off the offensive. His commanders added a plea that he lower his strategic sights, abandoning the drive to Antwerp and concentrating on the destruction by 5th and 6th Panzer Armies of the Allied formations to the east of the River Meuse, the 'small solution' reasserting itself. Hitler, however, was not in a mood to be coaxed away from the

Above: A knocked-out King Tiger tank, still alight, is passed by an American patrol in the northern sector of the Ardennes. It is likely that the tank has been caught in the open and destroyed by a rocket from an Allied fighter-bomber.

unattainable prize of Antwerp. He agreed to confine the offensive to the east of the Meuse, but only as a temporary measure. Once the Americans had been worked over, he would resume the dash for Antwerp. Above all, Bastogne, and the road network radiating from it, must be secured.

This flight from reality contrasted starkly with the German experience on the ground. One of the German Army's élite divisions, 2nd SS Panzer *Das Reich* had been heavily involved in the fighting at Baraque de Fraiture and Manhay. The diary kept by an officer in on of its Panzergrenadier battalions records the mood on Christmas Day:

'With panzer support, we drive the enemy out of his positions. He withdraws slowly towards Manhay and Grandmenil under the cover of a barrage fired by hundreds of guns. There is absolutely no cover. Our guns in an orgy of spendthrift recklessness reply with eight rounds – and then cease fire. We have to save ammunition. But the order to attack has raised our spirits. It is much better than lying about in slit trenches in the cold subject to the enemy's savage bombardments. Some men are brought back suffering from frostbite. There are not enough felt boots to go round. During the evening the enemy is driven out of Manhay and Grandmenil and for tonight at least we have dry billets. We are guarded only by a thin outpost line on the edge of the village ... An attack has been ordered for tomorrow. The objective is Mormont. This means we have to be in position in good time. But the tanks and artillery have almost no fuel or ammunition left.'

On 29 December, Major-General F.W. von Mellenthin was on his way to take up a new appointment with 9th Panzer Division, travelling through the wooded hills northwest of Houffalize in the centre of the Ardennes salient. He later wrote: 'The icebound roads glistened in the sunshine and I witnessed the uninterrupted air attacks on our traffic routes and supply dumps. Not a single German plane was in the air, innumerable vehicles were shot up and their blackened wrecks littered the roads.'

Hitler insisted that his embattled commanders slog on, and ordered a second attack southwards from the Saar. Codenamed 'Nordwind' (North Wind) and launched by Army Group G from the German-held pocket around the city of Colmar, it was intended to force Patton to divert the divisions that were threatening the southern flank of the Ardennes salient, and thus enable 'Autumn Mist' to be resumed. 'North Wind' had been anticipated by US 6th Army Group intelligence, which had warned Eisenhower and the Army Group commander, General Jacob Devers. Eisenhower suggested to Devers that he withdraw from the sector rather than risk encirclement. This suggestion carried with it one political drawback: the loss of the Alsatian city of Strasbourg, which had been liberated by troops of French 1st Army in November 1944 after remaining under German control from 1870 to 1918 and then again from 1940. The French were understandably concerned that the returning Germans would exact reprisals on Strasbourg's civilian population. They threatened to ignore Eisenhower and defend the city.

Churchill was called in to discuss the thorny problem at Versailles with Eisenhower, the leader of the Free French, General de Gaulle, and General Alphonse Juin, Chief of Staff to the French National Defence Committee. It was decided to bow to French wishes and leave the city within the area to be defended by the Allies.

In the event, the German threat to Strasbourg was shortlived, and 'North Wind' blew itself out within a week without posing any threat to the Allied dispositions. However, Hitler had a final card up his sleeve: Operation 'Bodenplatte' ('Base Plate'), an attack by the *Luftwaffe* on Allied tactical airfields. The operation had its origins in a meeting held on 15 December 1944, the day before the launch of 'Autumn Mist', at the headquarters of *Jagdkorps* (Fighter Corps) 2 near Altkirchen. Here the commander of Fighter Corps 2, Major-General Dietrich Pelz, outlined a plan to attack the 16 Allied tactical airfields in the Low Countries and northeast France. However, the bad weather that accompanied the opening of 'Autumn Mist' meant that it was not until 31 December that *Luftwaffe* fighter commanders were given the go-ahead for the operation. But by then it was too late. Nevertheless, the preparations were thorough: there had been extensive photo-reconnaissance of the targets and each pilot was given a 1:500000 scale map with his route approach drawn in. Smoke flares would mark turning points and marker rockets would indicate the German front line. Each formation would be guided to the target by a Ju 88 pathfinder.

The 600 aircraft mustered for 'Base Plate' took off on the morning of 1 January at times synchronized to ensure simultaneous attacks at 09:20 hours. The operation achieved a measure of surprise and accounted for some 150 Allied aircraft destroyed on the ground. However, during the operation the *Luftwaffe* lost 214 pilots, including many instructors and 18 experienced commanders, who at this stage in the war were irreplaceable. The pilot losses incurred by Allied 2nd Tactical Air Force were 15. Total German aircraft losses, including those downed by friendly fire, were 300. Allied losses in 'Base Plate' represented just 0.5 per cent of the aircraft available to the Supreme Headquarters Allied Expeditionary Force (SHAEF). The German losses were nearly 30 per cent of the strike force painfully amassed for the operation at the cost of denuding other fronts of air support.

At the end of December, the Allies moved on to the offensive in the Ardennes salient. West of Bastogne, VIII Corps, spearheaded by 11th Armored Division, drove north towards Houffalize. The following day and to the east of Bastogne, III Corps, led by 6th Armored Division, struck northeast towards St Vith. Both drives hit strong resistance and slow progress was compounded by icy roads, which made armour unmanageable, while bad weather once again deprived the Allies of air support.

By 1 January there were eight German divisions in the Bastogne sector, and while VIII and III Corps pushed north, they remained determined to take the town, the retention of which by the Americans had

Above: Junkers Ju 88 bombers similiar to those used as pathfinders for Operation 'Base Plate', a last-ditch attempt to disrupt the all-powerful Allied air cover which was proving so efficient in hunting down German targets of opportunity.

Below: Hitler with Speer, Jodl and Keitel in January 1945. Whistling in the wind, the Führer convinced himself that the Ardennes offensive had brought about a 'great easing of the situation'. In fact it had been an unmitigated disaster, from which the Allies soon recovered.

fatally unhinged 'Autumn Mist'. In turn, the German formations dislocated the northward thrust by VIII and III Corps. The threat to Bastogne was not removed until 4 January.

On 3 January Rundstedt had informed his commanders that the only sensible course of action was to withdraw from the Ardennes salient and save as much equipment and as many men as possible. The same day, the northern claw of the Allied pincer began to close as 1st Army went on to the attack on a 48km (35-mile) front, and elements of XXX Corps attacked from the west. Again, the troops found the

Above: The results of Operation 'Base Plate' on 1 January 1945, the last throw of the Luftwaffe. *It achieved surprise and destroyed 150 Allied aircraft, but the loss of experienced* Luftwaffe *pilots could not be made good. For the Allies it was a hiccup; for the* Luftwaffe *a disaster.*

going tough. The enemy was well organized with dug-in tanks and antitank guns, and the weather was appalling, limiting visibility to 183m (200yd) and the pace of the advance to a gruelling crawl of around 3km (2 miles) on the first day, and halting it thereafter for another two days.

On 5 January, Hitler finally abandoned his lingering hopes of taking Bastogne, and three days later he issued Model with an authorization to give up the area which lay west of Houffalize. German troops were now withdrawn from the tip of the salient. This was a signal that 'Autumn Mist' was a lost cause. However, the Führer still refused to sanction a complete withdrawal behind the West Wall. With the return of good flying weather, this exposed the German formations to further punishment from the punishing Allied fighter-bombers.

After the war, Manteuffel recalled how close the German Army came to annihilation, recording that that by 5 January 'the situation was so serious that I feared Montgomery would cut off all our armies. Although we managed to avoid this danger, a large part of them was sacrificed. Our losses were much

heavier in this later stage than they had been earlier, owing to Hitler's policy of "no withdrawal". It spelt bankruptcy because we could not afford such losses.'

On 13 January, the American 82nd and the British 1st Airborne Divisions finally managed to make contact in what had been the centre of the Ardennes salient. And on 16 December, 1st and 3rd Armies joined hands at Houffalize to close the pincers across the Bulge. Eisenhower now ordered 1st Army to revert to Bradley's command; however, 9th Army would remain under the control of Montgomery.

As the men of 3rd Army's 11th Armored Division and 1st Army's 2nd Division moved into Houffalize, General Patton and his driver Sergeant Mims were motoring up to join them. At one point Patton ordered Mims to stop. He wanted to investigate something which had caught his eye: what appeared to be a long row of dark twigs projecting above the surface of the snow. On closer inspection they proved to be the toes of soldiers whose boots had been removed, after they had fallen, by other soldiers. It was a 'nasty sight', as Patton would later tell his staff officers. The last spasm of fighting in the Ardennes salient seemed to have been fought in a gigantic refrigerator that turned soldiers' corpses the colour of claret.

With the Battle of the Bulge all but won, Montgomery further inflamed relations within the

Above: Fuel bowsers blaze at one of the Allied airfields attacked in Operation 'Base Plate'. Allied air losses represented just 0.5 per cent of the aircraft available to Eisenhower; German losses were one-third of the forces amassed for the operation.

Allied High Command. Egotistically he claimed at a press conference on 7 January virtually the entire credit for the victory: 'The battle has been most interesting; I think possibly one of the most interesting and tricky … I have ever handled.'

Winston Churchill was obliged to mollify the outraged Americans with a generous speech in the House of Commons on 18 January in which the Prime Minister declared: 'the United States troops have done almost all the fighting and have suffered almost all the losses … Care must be taken not to claim for the British Army an undue share of what is undoubtedly the greatest American battle of the War, and will, I believe, be regarded an ever-famous American victory.'

Hitler had, nevertheless, given the Allies a tremendous, albeit temporary, shock in mid-December 1944. The threat of assassination by Skorzeny's Greif commandos had caused Eisenhower to surround himself with bodyguards. The threat to Allied troops had forced him briefly to contemplate sending black American troops, who had been previously strictly segregated, into action alongside whites in fully integrated units. Hitler consoled himself with the thought that 'Autumn Mist' had shaken the optimism of the Western Allies' political leaders, producing 'a tremendous easing of the situation … the enemy has had to abandon all his plans for the attack. He has

been obliged to regroup his forces. He has had to throw in again units which were fatigued. He is severely criticized at home … Already he has had to admit that there is no chance of the war being ended before August, perhaps not before the end of next year.'

Between 16 December and 16 January, 5th and 6th Panzer Armies had inflicted some 10,200 fatal casualties on US 12th Army Group and taken 15,000 American prisoners. Nevertheless, 'Autumn Mist' had merely caused a hiccup in the Allied preparations to break into Germany, at the expense, to the Germans, of denying to the *Ostheer* the men and materiel desperately needed on the Eastern Front. In the last two months of 1944, 2299 tanks and assault guns and 18 new divisions had been committed to the West but only 920 tanks and 5 divisions to the East, where the *Ostheer* faced 225 Red Army rifle divisions, 22 tank corps and 29 other armoured formations, with only 133 divisions, 30 of which were threatened with encirclement in the Baltic.

The remnants of Dietrich's 6th Panzer Army were sent to the Eastern Front, where a renewed Red

Army offensive had burst upon the *Ostheer* on 12 January. In the Ardennes, the men of 6th Army left behind 100,000 men of the *Westheer* either killed, wounded or captured, plus 800 tanks and 1000 aircraft destroyed. None of these losses, human or material, could be made good. Hitler's 'last gamble' (as 'Autumn Mist' came to be dubbed), had bought

Below: American GIs rest near Malmédy on their way to the front lines. For the Allies the German offensive had come as an unpleasant surprise, but they soon regained the initiative, thanks in no small part to the vital efforts of Allied airpower once the skies had cleared.

a little time at great cost. The operation had also failed in its objective of destroying 30 Allied divisions and inflicting a second Dunkirk on the British. Furthermore, it had won back no ground at all.

The battle in the Ardennes had been fought largely because of mistaken assumptions made by the Allied and German High Commands. At the beginning of December, the Allies had convinced themselves that Germany was effectively finished and lacked the resources to mount another offensive in the West. In reaching this conclusion, they had assumed that the conduct of German operations still rested in the

Above: An American infantryman escorts a German column into captivity. Hitler's Third Reich had only five months to live – the Ardennes offensive had thrown away precious reserves of fuel, men and matériel in a futile attempt to turn back the clock to the successes of 1940.

hands of the rational and professional Rundstedt. However, the opposite was true here. The planning and execution of 'Autumn Mist' lay entirely with the irrational and dangerously detached Adolf Hitler. When Rundstedt received his final orders, the words 'Not To Be Altered' were scrawled on them in the Führer's spidery hand.

But Allied intelligence chose to ignore evidence which did not fit the picture it had formed of German capabilities and intentions. It also chose to underestimate the powers of recovery and remarkable fighting qualities displayed by the German Army in this last spasm of the war in the West.

For his part, Hitler had gambled on what he perceived as the flawed nature of the troops and the alliance arrayed against him in Western Europe. However, the cracks that did open up – notably those between Montgomery and his American counterparts – were not fatal to the alliance against Nazi Germany, nor to the conduct of operations in the Ardennes, as is evidenced by Eisenhower's decision to give Montgomery operational control of Allied

forces on the northern side of the Bulge. Montgomery knew that Ike was no 'fighting general', like Patton or himself, but what he failed to appreciate was Eisenhower's formidable diplomatic skills, which enabled the Supreme Commander to weld such antithetical elements into a formidable and ultimately winning fighting alliance.

On 7 December 1944, Eisenhower was motoring through the Ardennes on the way to a meeting with Montgomery. Gazing at the wooded country around him, he observed that the Allies might be in for 'a nasty little Kasserine'. This was a reference to the battle in North Africa in February 1943, when the inexperienced US II Corps was given a drubbing by 5th Panzer Army. But there was to be no repetition in the Ardennes. Here, American troops won their greatest victory in the European war.

Order of Battle

Supreme Headquarters Allied Expeditionary Force (SHAEF)

GENERAL OF THE ARMY
Dwight D. Eisenhower

US ARMY
(1 JANUARY 1945)

12 US ARMY GROUP
Lieutenant-General
Omar N. Bradley

US 1ST ARMY
(Lieutenant-General
Courtney H. Hodges)
V CORPS (Major-General
Leonard T. Gerow)
1 Infantry Division ('Big Red
One', Brigadier-General
Clift Andrus)
2 Infantry Division
('Indianhead',
Major-General
Walter M. Robertson)
9 Infantry Division
('Octofoil', Major-
General Louis A. Craig)
78 Infantry Division
('Lightning', Major-
General Edwin P.
Parker Jr)
99 Infantry Division
('Checkerboard', Major-
General Walter E. Lauer)
VII CORPS (Major-General
Joseph Lawton Collins)
2 Armored Division ('Hell on
Wheels', Major-General
Ernest N. Harmon)
3 Armored Division
('Spearhead', Major-
General Maurice Rose
83 Infantry Division
('Thunderbolt',
Brigadier-General
Alexander R. Bolling)
84 Infantry Division
('Railsplitter',
Brigadier-General
Alexander R. Bolling)
XVIII *Airborne Corps*
(Major-General Matthew
B. Ridgway)
7 Armored Division ('Lucky
Seventh', Brigadier-
General Robert W.

Hasbrouck)
30 Infantry Division ('Old
Hickory'. Major-General
Leland S. Hobbs)
75 Infantry Division (Major-
General
Fay B. Prickett)
82 Airborne Division ('All
American', Major-
General James M. Gavin
106 Infantry Division
('Golden Lions', Major-
General Alan W. Jones)

US 3RD ARMY
(LIEUTENANT-GENERAL
George S. Patton Jr)
III CORPS (Major-General
John Millikins)
4 Armored Division (Major-
General
Hugh J. Gaffey
6 Armored Division ('Super
Sixth', Major-General
Robert W.Grow
26 Infantry Division
('Yankee', Major-
General Willard S.Paul)
35 Infantry Division ('Santa
Fe', Major-General Paul
W. Baade)
90 Infantry Division ('Tough
Hombres', Major-
General
James A. Van Fleet)
VIII CORPS (Major-General
Troy H. Middleton)
9 Armored Division (Major-
General
John W. Leonard)
11 Armored Division
('Thunderbolt',
Brigadier-General
Charles S. Kilburn)
17 Airborne Division
('Golden Talon', Major-
General William M.
Miley)
28 Infantry Division
('Keystone', Major-
General Norman D. Cota)
87 Infantry Division
('Golden Acorn',
Brigadier-General Frank
L. Culin Jr)
101 Airborne Division
('Screaming Eagles',
Brigadier-General

Anthony C. McAuliffe
(acting))
XII CORPS (Major-General
Manton S. Eddy)
4 Infantry Division ('Ivy',
Major-General Raymond
O. Barton)
5 Infantry Division ('Red
Diamond', Major-
General S.Leroy Irwin)
10 Armored Division ('Tiger',
Major-General William
H. H. Morris Jr)
80 Infantry Division ('Blue
Ridge', Major-General
Horace L. McBride)

US ARMY AIR FORCES

US STRATEGIC AIR FORCES IN EUROPE
General Carl Spaatz

8 Air Force
(Lieutenant-General
James H. Doolittle)
9 Air Force
(Lieutenant-General
Hoyt S. Vandenberg)
9 Bombardment Division
(Major-General Samuel
E. Anderson)
9 Troop Carrier Command
(Major-General
Paul L. Williams)
9 Tactical Air Command
(supporting 1 Army,
Major-General
Elwood R. Quesada)
19 Tactical Air Command
(supporting 3 Army,
Brigadier-General
Otto P. Weyland)
29 Tactical Air Command
(supporting 9 Army,
Major-General
Richard E. Nugent)

BRITISH ARMY

21 ARMY GROUP
Field Marshal Sir
Bernard L. Montgomery

XXX CORPS
(Lieutenant-General
Brian G. Horrocks)

6 Airborne Division (Major-
General
Eric L. Bols)
51 Infantry Division
(Highland, Major-
General T.G. Rennie)
53 Infantry Division (Welsh,
Major-General R.K.
Ross)
29 Armoured Brigade
(Brigadier-General
C.B.C. Harvey)
33 Armoured Brigade
(Brigadier-General H.B.
Scott)
34 Amy Tank Brigade
(Brigadier-General
W.S. Clarke)

*(In reserve, 43 and 50 Infantry
Divisions and Guards
Armoured Division)*

ROYAL AIR FORCE

BOMBER COMMAND
Air Chief Marshal
Sir Arthur T. Harris

FIGHTER COMMAND
Air Marshal
Sir Roderic M. Hill

2 TACTICAL AIR FORCE
AIR MARSHAL
Sir Arthur Coningham

WEHRMACHT
(28 DECEMBER 1944)

OB WEST
Field Marshal
Gerd von Rundstedt

ARMY GROUP B
Field Marshal
Walter Model

5 PANZER ARMY
(General Hasso von
Manteuffel)
47 Panzer Corps (General
Heinrich von Luttwitz)
2 Panzer Division (Colonel
Meinrad von Lauchert)
9 Panzer Division (Major-
General Harald von
Elverfeldt)

Panzer Lehr Division
(Lieutenant-General
Fritz Bayerlein)
26 Volksgrenadier Division
(Colonel Heinz Kokott)
Fuhrer Begleit Brigade
(Colonel Otto Remer)
66 CORPS
(General Walter Lucht)
18 Volksgrenadier Division
(Colonel Hoffman-
Schonborn)
62 Volksgrenadier Division
(Colonel Friedrich Kittel)
58 Panzer Corps
(General Walter Kruger)
116 Volksgrenadier Division
(Major-General Siegfried
von Walenburg)
560 Volksgrenadier Division
(Colonel Rudolf
Langhauser)
29 Panzer Corps (Lieutenant-
General Karl Decker)
167 Volksgrenadier Division
(Lieutenant-General
Hans-Kurt Hocker)

6 PANZER ARMY
(SS General
Sepp Dietrich)
I SS Panzer Corps
(SS General Hermann
Priess)
1 SS Panzer Division
(*LEIBSTANDARTE* Adolf
Hitler, SS Colonel
Wilhelm Mohnke)
3 Parachute Division (Major-
General Wadehn)
12 SS Panzer Division (*HITLER
JUGEND*, Colonel Hugo
Kraas)
12 Volksgrenadier Division
(Major-General Gerhard
Engel)
277 Volksgrenadier Division
(Colonel Wilhelm
Viebig)
150 Panzer Brigade
(Lieutenant-Colonel
Otto Skorzeny)
II SS Panzer Corps (General
Willi Bittrich)
2 SS Panzer Division (*DAS
REICH*, Major-General
Heinz Lammerding)
9 SS Panzer Division

(*HOHENSTAUFEN*, Brigadier
Sylvester Stadler)
67 CORPS (Lieutenant-
General Otto Hitzfeld)
3 Panzergrenadier Division
(Major-General Walter
Denkert)
245 Volksgrenadier Division
(Colonel Peter Koerte)
272 Volksgrenadier Division
(Colonel Georg
Kosmalla)
326 Volksgrenadier Division
(Colonel Erwin
Kaschner)

7 ARMY
(General Erich
Brandenberger)
53 Corps (General von
Rothkirch und Trach)
9 Volksgrenadier Division
(Colonel Werner Kolb)
15 Panzergrenadier Division
(Colonel
Hans-Joachim Deckett)
Führer Grenadier Brigade
(Colonel Hans-Joachim
Kahler)
80 CORPS

(General Franz Beyer)
212 Volksgrenadier Division
Major-General Franz
von Sensfuss)
276 Volksgrenadier Division
(General Kurt Mohring,
later Colonel Hugo
Dempwolff)
340 Volksgrenadier Division
(Colonel Theodor
Tolsdorff)
85 CORPS
(General Baptist Kniess)
5 Parachute Division
(Colonel Ludwig
Heilmann)
352 Volksgrenadier Division
(Colonel Erich Schmidt)
79 Volksgrenadier Division
(Colonel Alois Weber)

LUFTWAFFE

II FIGHTER CORPS
Major-General Dietrich
Peltz

III FLAK CORPS
Lieutenant-General
Wolfgang Pickert

SELECTED READING LIST

Bradley, Omar N, *A Soldier's Story,* Henry Holt (1951).
Colbaugh, Jack, *The Bloody Patch: A True Story of the Daring 28th Infantry Division,* Vantage Press (1973).
Cole, Hugh M., *The Ardennes: Battle of the Bulge,* Washington DC Govt Printing Office (1965).
Cole, Hugh M., *The Lorraine Campaign,* Washington DC Govt Printing Office (1950).
Cooper, Matthew, *The German Army 1939–1945,* Macdonald and Janes (1978).
De Guingand, Major-General Sir F., *Operation Victory,* Hodder and Stoughton (1947).
Dupuy, Colonel R. Ernest, *Lion in the Way: the 106th Infantry Division in World War II,* Infantry Journal Press (1949).
Eisenhower, Dwight D., *Crusade in Europe,* Doubleday (1948).
Elstob, Peter, *Hitler's Last Offensive,* Secker and Warburg (1971).
Gavin, James M., *On to Berlin: Battles of an Airborne Commander 1943–1946,* Viking (1978).
Guderian, Heinz, *Panzer Leader,* Futura (1987).
Harmon, Major-General E.N., *Combat Commander: Autobiography of a Soldier,* Prentice Hall (1970).
Jacobson H.A. (ed), *Decisive Battles of World War II: The German View,* Putnam (1965).
Kreipe, General Werner, *The Kreipe Diary 22 July–2 November 1944,* Office of the Chief of Military History US Army (unpublished diary).
Lauer, Major-General Walter E., *Battle Babies: The Story of 99th Infantry Division in World War II,* Military Press

of Louisiana (1951).
Liddell Hart, Basil, *The Other Side of the Hill,* Cassell (1978).
Lucas, James, *Das Reich,* Cassell (1991).
MacDonald, Charles B, *The Battle of the Bulge,* Weidenfeld and Nicholson (1984).
MacDonald, Charles B, *Company Commander,* Infantry Journal Press (1947).
MacDonald, Charles B., *The Last Offensive,* Washington DC Govt Printing Office (1973).
MacDonald, Charles B., *The Siegfried Line Campaign,* Washington DC Govt Printing Office (1963).
Mellenthin, General F.W., *German Generals of World War II: As I Saw Them,* Futura (1977).
Mellenthin, General F.W., *Panzer Battles,* Futura (1979).
Montgomery of Alamein, Field Marshal, *Normandy to the Baltic,* Hutchinson (1947).
Patton, George S. Jr, *War As I Knew It,* Houghton Mifflin (1947).
Pogue, Forrest C., *The Supreme Command,* Washington DC Govt Printing Office (1954).
Skorzeny, Otto, *Skorzeny's Secret Missions,* Dutton (1951).
Toland, John, *The Story of the Bulge,* Random House (1959).
Westphal, General Siegfried, *The German Army in the West,* Cassell (1951).
Whiting, Charles, *Massacre at Malmédy,* Stein and Day (1971).
Wykes, Alan, *SS Leibstandarte,* Ballantine (1974).

Index

Page numbers in *italics* indicate captions